MAKING

Hallelujah Hats!

Crafts and Activities Based on Bible Stories

by

Mary Doerfler-Dall

PAULIST PRESS
New York/Mahwah, N.J.

The scripture verses contained within are based on the New Revised Standard Version of the Bible, Oxford University Press.

Permission to copy the art and text in this book is granted to purchasers for classroom or family use at no charge.

Cover design by Cheryl Nathan

Cover and interior photography by Heidi Bratton

ISBN: 0–8091–3788–7

Published by Paulist Press
997 Macarthur Boulevard
Mahwah, New Jersey 07430

Printed and bound in the
United States of America

CONTENTS

Dedication

For Dominic
May he find **Making Hallelujah Hats!**
an important part of his early religious training.

Acknowledgements

Thanks to my parents, Henry and Mary,
who always served as loving, living examples of Christian principles.

Thanks to the many CCD and Sunday School teachers along the way who
inspired; especially John and Maureen Doerfler, who helped in story selection.

Special thanks to my husband, Dan, for his constant strength and support.

Thanks also to our three children Erin, Amanda and Mike who are always a source
of revitalization and encouragement.

Thanks to editor Karen Scialabba for her invaluable wisdom, guidance and insight
that expanded and strengthened the project.

INTRODUCTION

MAKING HALLELUJAH HATS! is a new and fun way to learn about the wonderful stories of the Bible. It combines children's love for stories, hats and puppet shows into one unique hands-on approach to learning about the Bible.

The materials for completing the hat and puppet projects are inexpensive and readily available. Bible stories are provided in simple language for today's children and, by means of the reference given on the page, can be used as a stepping stone to the authorized Bible. Remind the children of simple safety rules and watch as they begin to "experience" Bible stories. (*Note:* The suggested "Time required" for completion is for hat assembly only.)

A lesson plan connects the craft to the story, making the ideas and goals of the lesson more visual and memorable for the child. The plan also helps to expand the craft, enabling the child to see how the Bible applies to their world today.

Ideas to make each project even more special will show you how to enjoy and customize these crafts for children of all ages.

Making Hallelujah Hats! brings the Bible to life for your child.

HOW TO USE THIS BOOK

- Reproduce the pattern pieces

- Read the stories

- Use the helpful lesson plan

- Children can follow the step-by-step instructions

- Enhance your project by using "special" suggestions

- Share your project *and* your love of the Bible

MATERIALS

Construction Paper	Staples/Stapler	Markers
Crayons	Tape	Glue/Paste
Scissors	Brass Fastener	Yarn/String/Thread
Hole Punch	Paints	Pencils

Optional materials: Glitter, Feathers, Stones, Fabric Scraps, et cetera.

TIPS FOR TEACHERS AND PARENTS

- Even if pieces are stored in an envelope, children's names or initials should be put on the backs of all pieces.

- While each project can be reproduced on standard copy paper, construction paper may be used throughout. Specific colors can then be used for specific items, (i.e., blue for water) and light colors can be used for pieces intended to be colored or painted.

- Color/paint smaller pieces first, then cut out.

- Color/paint band part of project prior to cutting. Once cut, small items such as feathers, glitter, stones, et cetera can more easily be added.

- If staples are used to secure the band, cover the pointed, sharp ends with a piece of clear tape to protect little heads.

- *An adult* may more easily cut slots for specific hat/puppet shows with a single blade type instrument.

- Sending a copy of the story home with the child will provide parental or sibling involvement as the story is reread and shared.

1. THE CREATION

Based on Genesis 1:1-31;2:1-4

Materials

Crayons
Markers or Paints
Scissors
Glue/Staples
Tape

Time required: 30–35 minutes

Directions

1. Read story and review lesson.
2. Color pieces. Cut out.
3. Glue "night" (black) and "day" (blue) pieces of sky together at center.
4. Glue the **edges only** of the hands-cloud piece. Attach to sky piece (centering).
5. Use rolled tape pieces to place items on the world. Glue in place if permanency is required.
6. When hands-cloud piece is dry, slip world into "pocket" that is created.
7. Adjust band to fit, using the cloud to connect the blue and black pieces at back.

Suggestions

- Add pulled cotton balls to the clouds. Add small wisps of cotton balls to the sky sections.
- Glitter the sun, moon and star.
- Small pictures from magazines can be added to items on the globe.
- A small picture of the child may be cut out and added.
- Add small feathers or bits of live greenery or small pebbles to world.
- Glue an envelope to the inside of band, sky section, to hold the pieces.

To Make This Craft Special...

★ Ask each child what he or she would add to the world that is not in this lesson. (i.e., some additional animals, plants or other things to make it more personal.)

★ Sing "He's Got the Whole World in His Hands." Use the song to promote a finger play adding new items as you go along (i.e., "He's got the big yellow sun in His hands....He's got the trees and the flowers in His hands, et cetera")

★ Write "thank-you notes" to God. Have each child cite something in the world that is personally special.

★ If *The Creation* is to be used as a hat only, glue the pieces in place.

Send Home

• Send the story *The Creation* home with each child so that the sharing and retelling of the story can continue.

• Roll the story and hold it closed with a special sticker that shows the greatness of God. Or fold it and tuck it into God's hands along with the world.

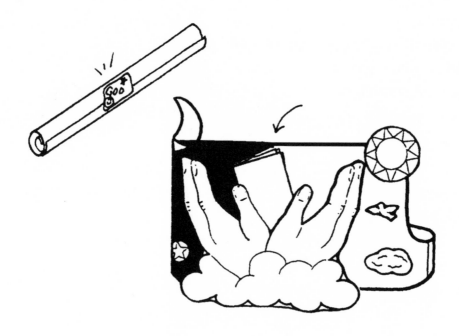

THE CREATION
Based on Genesis 1:1-31;2:1-4

In the beginning, God made the heavens and the earth. There was nothing but darkness all around and wind swept over the water.

Then, God said, "Let there be light!" God saw that the light was good. God divided the light from the darkness. The light was called Day and the dark was called Night. This was the first day.

On the second day, God made a dome and called it the Sky.

On the third day, God said, "Let the waters gather together and let dry land appear." The land became the Earth; the water became the Seas. Next, God made wonderful things grow from the earth—all sorts of beautiful plants. God saw that this was good.

Then, on the fourth day, God made two great lights: the sun for day and the moon for night. God made millions and millions of stars, placing them in the heavens to shine. Again God saw how good it was.

On the fifth day, God looked to the water, creating every living thing in the sea, from the smallest creature to the greatest sea monsters. Next, God looked to the sky, creating all the flying birds. God blessed the creatures, telling them, "Go forth; fill up the waters and the sky." God saw that this was good.

On the sixth day, God said, "Let the earth be filled with living creatures: cattle, creeping things and wild animals of every kind." And it was so. God saw that it was good. God looked around at all the beautiful things and all the wonderful creatures on the land, in the water and in the sky. Then, God said, "Let us make people! They will be in charge of the fish, the birds, the cattle, the wild animals and the creeping, crawling creatures of the earth. They will be special to me."

God created man and woman. They were made in the image of God. God blessed them, saying, "Fill up the earth. Rule over it. I have given you plants, trees, birds, animals and all living creatures."

Now, on the seventh day, God was finished with the work of creation and rested. God blessed the seventh day and made it holy.

This is the story of God and creation.

God made all things!

LESSON PLAN

Objectives:

1. To develop an understanding that everything in the universe was created by God and given to us.
2. To understand the concept of measuring time.
3. To develop an appreciation of nature and an appreciation of our creator.
4. To follow general and specific directions.
5. To _____.

Theme: All things come from God. He gives us a world to share. We are thankful for the world he gave us.

Preparation:

Let's consider the idea of creation. We will all hold a small ball of clay. Now, let's knead it in our hands and then shape it into a ball. Can you cradle the ball? Just as each of us can knead this clay, God holds and molds all of us individually and in a special way. God holds us, even though we cannot see God or God's hands.

Read the story *The Creation.*

Discuss/Ask:

Did you ever think of all the things God has given to us? Do you realize that everything in the world was made by God for us? Let's list some of the things in the world for which we are thankful to God.

How can we show God we are thankful for this world that He has given us?

Explain:

We must take care of each other and we must take care of our earth. Just as we should not harm our cities and towns with garbage and poisonous toxins, we must not hurt our neighbors, friends and families. We should show kindness.

Follow Directions for Craft.

THE CREATION

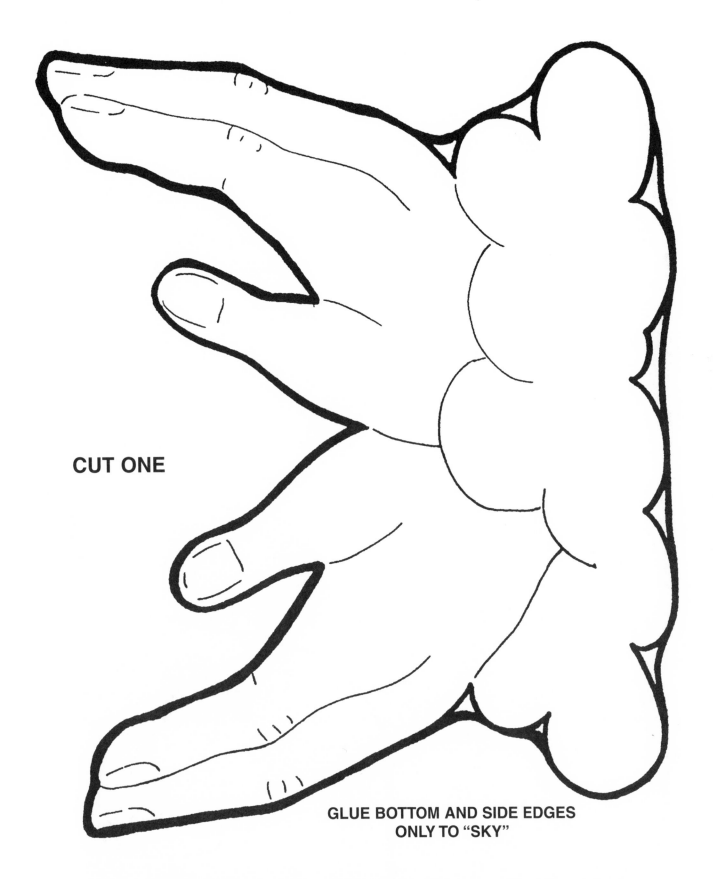

CUT ONE

GLUE BOTTOM AND SIDE EDGES
ONLY TO "SKY"

WHEN HANDS ARE DRY, TUCK WORLD INTO POCKET CREATED BY HANDS

THE CREATION

GLUE BLUE AND BLACK "SKY" PIECES TOGETHER HERE

FRONT I & II

SKY

BLACK   BLUE

CUT TWO
(ONE BLACK,
ONE BLUE)

ATTACH BACK WITH CLOUD, SIZING TO FIT

THE CREATION

CUT ONE EACH

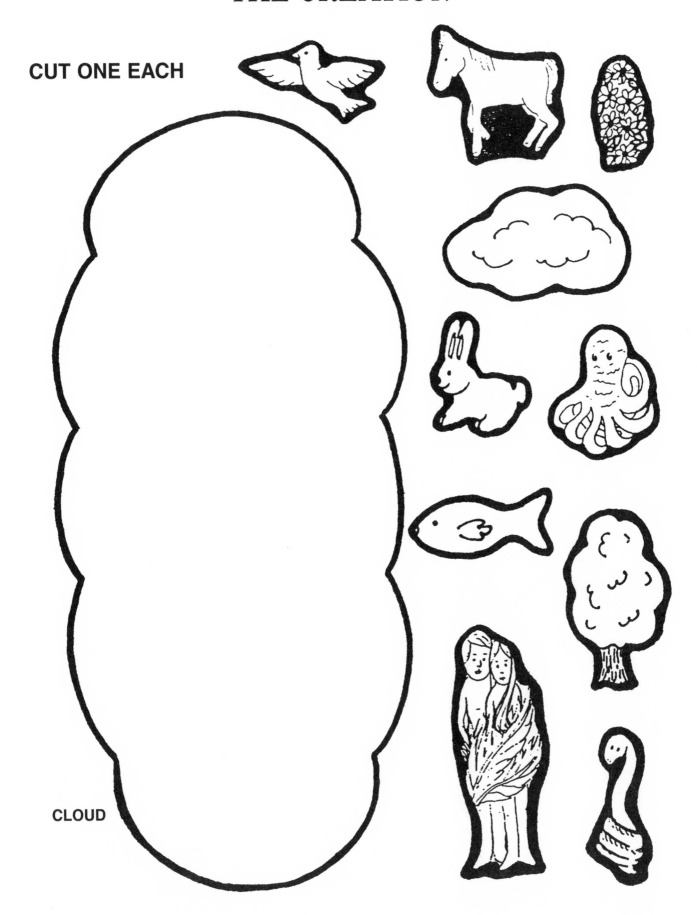

CLOUD

9

THE CREATION

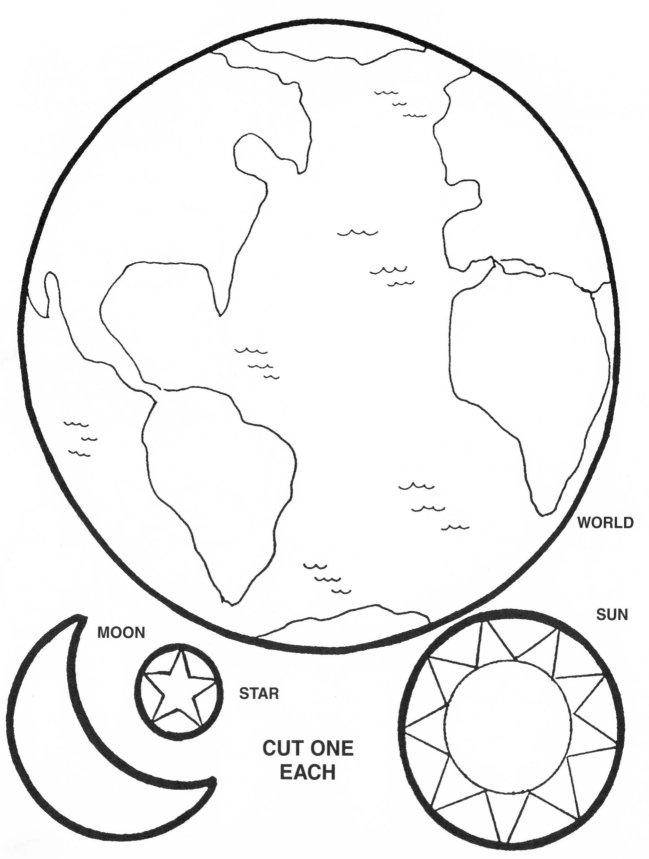

WORLD

SUN

MOON

STAR

CUT ONE
EACH

USING GLUE OR ROLLED TAPE, ATTACH
SUN, MOON AND STAR TO SKY SECTIONS

2. ADAM AND EVE

Based on Genesis 2;3

Materials

Crayons
Markers or Paints
Scissors
Glue/ Staples
Tape

Time required: 20–25 minutes

Directions

1. Read Story and review lesson.
2. Color pieces. Cut out.
3. Cut slit for snake.
4. Roll tape and attach apple to the tree.
5. Fold up front section. Glue at **edges only.**
6. Add the two other band pieces to front.
7. Adjust band to fit at back.
8. Glue the *bottom front* of bush so that it fits into the front slot. Make sure that it allows Adam and Eve to hide behind the bush.
9. Use rolled tape to hold Adam and Eve in the slot. (When banished, they can be placed behind the tree.)

Suggestions

- Add bright tissue paper pieces to the plants.
- Lightly glitter the tree.
- Add construction paper grass to the front section that is folded up.
- Add scraps of yarn to hair.
- Add a small yarn tongue to snake.

To Make This Craft Special...

★ Have the children act out the story. Use a plant on a desk as the "tree." An arm and hand can be a "snake" if eyes are drawn on the back of the hand.

★ If the project is to be used as a hat only, attach Adam and Eve to either side of the tree. Glue the bush in place. Lightly glue the snake's tail into the slot.

★ If the project is to be used as a puppet show only, glue the bush as shown and roll tape to hold Adam and Eve in place for transit. Place an envelope at the back of the tree to hold the pieces.

Send Home

• Send the story *Adam and Eve* home with each child so that the sharing and retelling of the story can continue.

• Prior to sending the story home, roll the page into a scroll and hold with apple-scented (or any "fruit"-scented) sticker. Note: You may wish to point out that the Bible only states the word *fruit,* but an apple has come to be the symbol for the story.

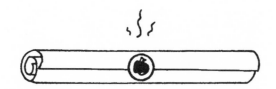

ADAM AND EVE
Based on Genesis 2;3

God made man. Then God took the man to live in the Garden of Eden. It was a rich and beautiful garden, full of everything the man could want. God told the man to take good care of the garden. God said, "You may eat from the trees." God pointed to a tree in the center of the garden and added, "But this one tree is not for you. It is a tree of good and evil. If you eat from this tree, you will die."

God thought about the man in the garden and said, "It is not good that the man should be alone." God wanted the man to have a partner as special as he was. So, the Lord made a woman. The man and woman, called Adam and Eve, lived happily together in the garden. Everything they needed was given to them by God.

Now, in the garden, there was a snake. The snake was the most clever animal God had made. One day the snake called to Eve and said: "Is it true that God will not let you eat fruit from the trees in this garden?"

Eve answered: "Oh, no. The garden is for us. We may eat the fruits." Then, she pointed to the tree of good and evil. "Only that one tree is not for us. If we eat from it, we will die."

The snake laughed at Eve and said, "Oh, nothing will happen. God knows that if you eat of this tree your eyes will see many new things. You will be like a god. Go ahead and eat from the tree. Doesn't the fruit look good?..."

Eve looked at the tree. It was beautiful and full of good fruit. Eve reached up and took some fruit from the tree. Then she ate it! Eve gave some of the fruit to Adam. He ate it too! Suddenly their eyes were opened. They saw that they had no clothes on their bodies. They made clothes for themselves out of leaves.

Adam and Eve were frightened. They heard God coming and they hid. The Lord called out to them. Finally Adam answered, "We are here. We were frightened since we had no clothes." God said, "You have disobeyed me! You have eaten from the tree of good and evil." Adam and Eve were sorry that they disobeyed God and could no longer live in the beautiful garden.

God punished the snake. From now on, it would have to crawl around on its belly. Then, God sent Adam and Eve out of the Garden of Eden. God told them they would have to grow their own food and work hard to live. They would now know good and evil. They would have to learn to live away from the Garden of Eden forever.

God loves us and gives us rules by which to live.

LESSON PLAN

Objectives:

1. To show that we should obey God in much the same way that children obey their parents.
2. To begin to understand the term "temptation."
3. To understand that God's rules are for our own protection.
4. To follow general and specific directions.
5. To _____.

Theme: God made man and woman. He gave them rules by which to live.

Preparation:

The story you are going to hear is about the first man and woman. God made man and woman and gave them a special place in which to live. God also gave them rules by which to live. He told them to obey his rules.

Read the story *Adam and Eve.*

Discuss/Ask:

Sometimes it is hard to obey rules. Do you ever have trouble doing what you are asked to do? What do you think about traffic laws, rules at school, rules at home, rules for when you go out to a restaurant, et cetera? Are these rules helpful? Why? Do we need these rules? What are some of God's rules for us?
Why did the serpent want Adam and Eve to eat the fruit from the forbidden tree? Do you think Adam and Eve were sorry they disobeyed God?

Explain:

God has rules for all of us. He wants us to do good things and be kind to each other. When someone tries to make us do something that is wrong, we should not listen because it is the same as if a little serpent was tempting us to do wrong too. We saw that Adam and Eve were punished for disobeying. We will feel very badly about disobeying God.

Follow Directions for Craft.

ADAM AND EVE

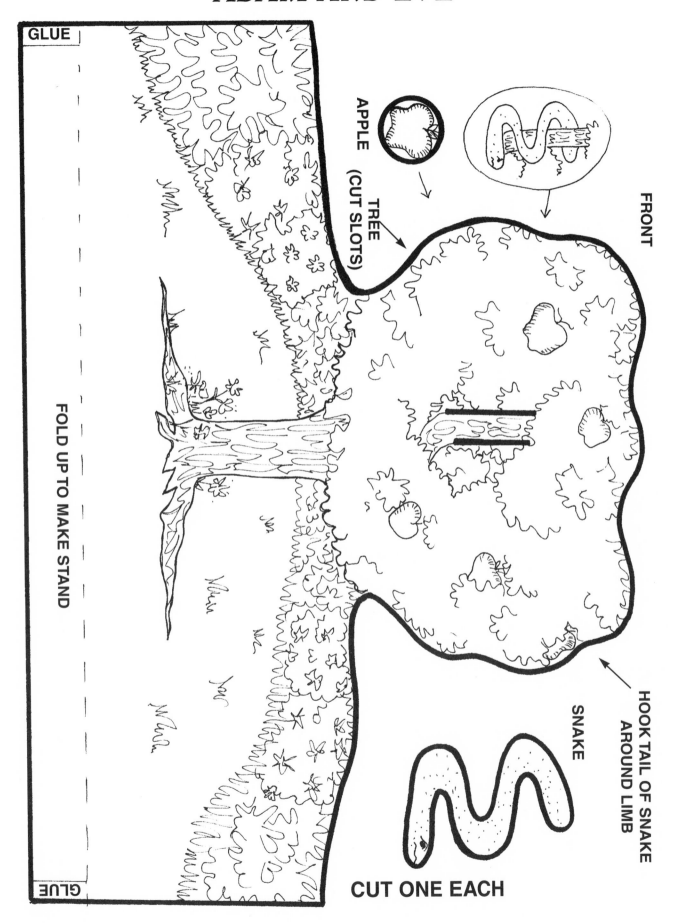

15

ADAM AND EVE

ADAM

EVE

CUT ONE EACH

CUT TWO

BUSH

SIDES

GLUE TO FRONT

GLUE TO FRONT

BUSH FRONT BOTTOM EDGE SHOULD BE GLUED TO INSIDE OF FRONT TRAY, ALLOWING ADAM AND EVE TO HIDE BEHIND THE BUSH

3. NOAH'S ARK

Based on Genesis 6:5–22;7;8;9

Materials

Crayons
Markers
Scissors
Tape
Glue

Time required: 25–30 minutes

Directions

1. Read story and review lesson.
2. Color pieces. Cut out. Make wave slot.
3. Size the headband sections and glue or tape together with the cut wave piece in front.
4. Cut the ark window on black lines only so that it will fold open.
5. Fold the ark in half and glue the inside **edges only.** (Allow edges to dry. All of the pieces will fit into the ark.)
6. Place the ark in the cut-out section of the wave.
7. Place all of the pieces inside the ark to transport home.

Suggestions

- Pieces of tissue paper, yarn, glitter can be used to enhance the water.
- Additional magazine pictures of animals can be cut out to go in the ark.
- Children can draw sea life in the water.
- Children can glue tiny scraps of cloth to the clothing.

To Make This Craft Special...

★ Play and sing songs about Noah and the animals while children work on the project.

★ If *Noah's Ark* is to be used as a hat only, glue the ark in place.

★ When used as a stage setting, the headband can be turned inside out. This will aid stability and it will appear that water is all around.

★ When the band is inside out and the ark is in the wave, hold the band opposite the ark and shake up and down slightly. This will make the ark appear to be bobbing up and down in the water.

★ If the ark is to be used as a puppet show, roll a piece of tape to hold the ark in place for transit. All of the *Noah's Ark* pieces fit into the open window section of the ark for easy transport.

Send Home

• Send the story *Noah's Ark* home with each child so that the sharing and retelling of the story can continue.

• Roll the story and hold it closed with a sticker or ribbon to which a sprig of plant or a few leaves have been added to reinforce that God kept his promise to give back dry land to Noah and his family.

NOAH'S ARK
Based on Genesis 6:5–22;7;8;9

The Lord God looked down upon the earth. Many people had become wicked. The Lord was angry—angry enough to punish the world. Now the Lord did see one man who was kind and good and obeyed the law. The man's name was Noah. Noah and his family loved God.

God decided to send a great flood to destroy the earth. First, God spoke to Noah. God said, "Make an ark of wood. You and your family will go into the ark and be safe inside when I send a flood down on the world." God told Noah exactly how to build the ark. Noah did as God told him. He put rooms in the ark and covered the outside with pitch (a kind of tar) to keep the waters out. Again, God spoke to Noah, "Take animals into the ark, two of every kind, one male and one female." God told Noah to store food in the ark also. Noah obeyed the Lord.

Noah and his sons finished the ark and waited for God's command. When the time came, God told Noah and his family to climb into the ark and bring in the animals two-by-two. When they were all in the ark, it began to rain. It rained hard for forty days and forty nights. Soon water covered everything. But Noah and his family and the animals were safe inside the ark.

Finally it stopped raining. Noah sent a raven out into the sky. It could not find any land. Next Noah sent out a dove; it too could not find a place to land and returned to the ark. After seven days Noah sent out a dove. This time the dove returned with an olive branch in its beak. Noah could tell that the water was starting to go down. Once more, after seven days, Noah sent out a dove and this time the bird did not return. The land was beginning to dry out and the birds could now live in the trees.

Then God said to Noah, "Go out of the ark; you are safe." Noah and his family and all of the animals came out of the ark. They were happy to be on land again. Noah built an altar of praise to God. God told them to go out and fill the earth.

Glory to God!

LESSON PLAN

Objectives:

1. To develop an understanding that we should accept God's will.
2. To develop an understanding of the power of faith and prayer.
3. To understand that commitment and perseverance can "move mountains."
4. To follow general and specific directions.
5. To _____.

Theme: We should obey God and trust in him. He will always be with us to love and help us in hard times.

Preparation:

What must we do to live with God forever? Will God show us the way when we feel lost in our lives? If we are faithful to God, will he show us how to live better lives? If we believe in God, then we must show our faith by changing our lives to include loving and caring for our neighbors.

Read the story *Noah's Ark*.

Discuss/Ask:

Let's talk about Noah and his family. Do you think Noah was afraid to change his life forever? How do you think Noah's neighbors must have acted when they saw him building a big ark when it was warm and sunny and there was no large body of water nearby? So many people around Noah and his family were not obeying God; he probably felt outnumbered. Still, he continued to listen to God. Noah's faith in God gave him courage and comfort. God gave Noah exactly what he needed to survive. How can we show God we are faithful to him? Does God give us what we need right away?

Explain:

When you wish for something it doesn't always come true. If you have faith, pray and keep your promises to God, then God will help you find exactly what it is that you need to live in this world.

Follow Directions for Craft.

NOAH'S ARK

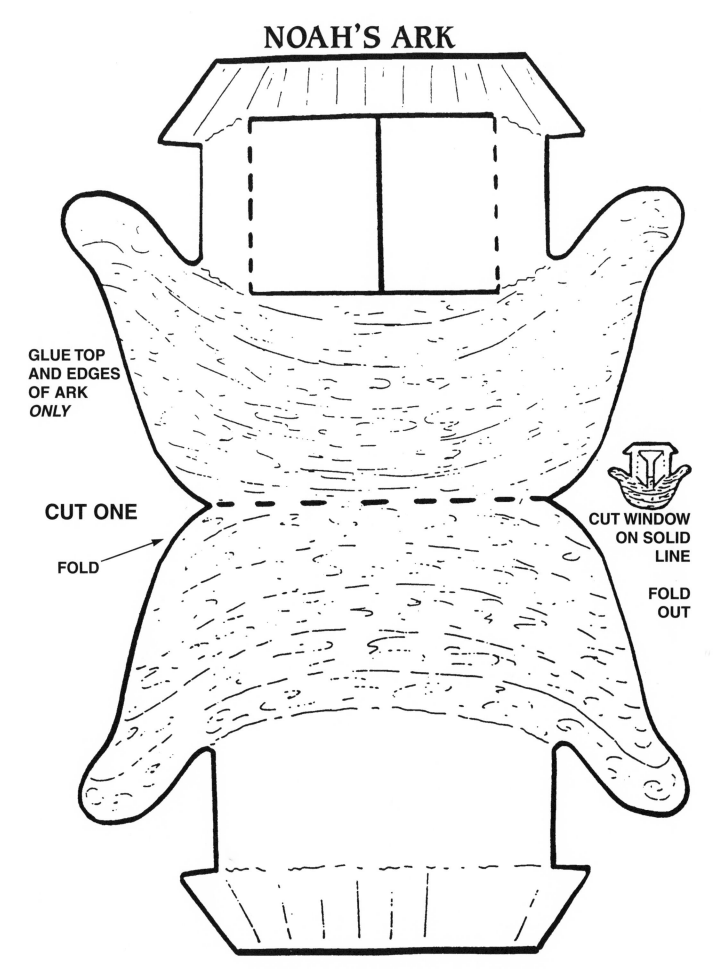

GLUE TOP
AND EDGES
OF ARK
ONLY

CUT ONE

FOLD

CUT WINDOW
ON SOLID
LINE

FOLD
OUT

NOAH'S ARK

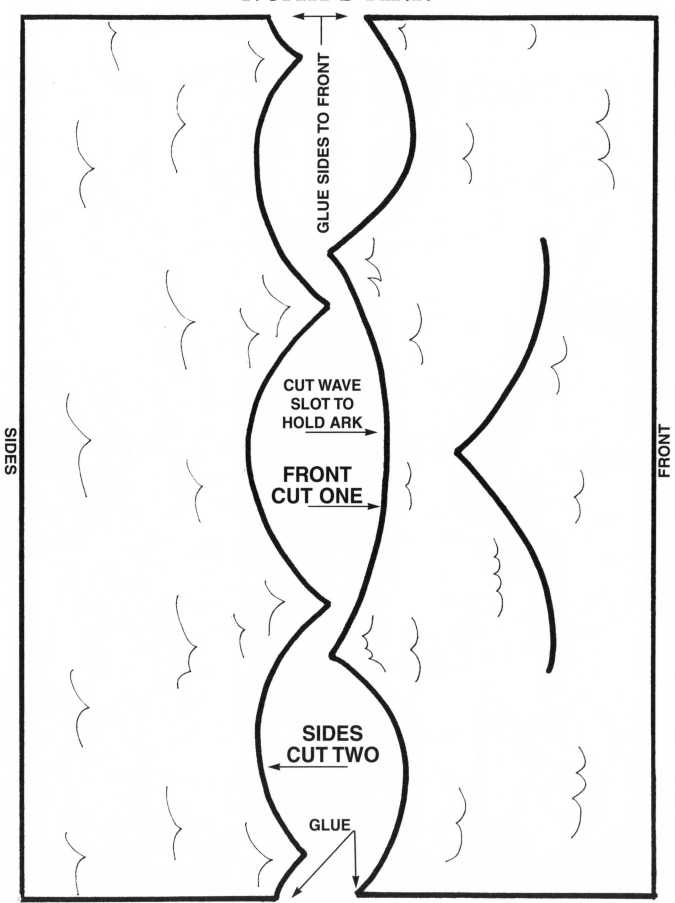

GLUE SIDES TO FRONT

CUT WAVE
SLOT TO
HOLD ARK

**FRONT
CUT ONE**

**SIDES
CUT TWO**

GLUE

SIDES

FRONT

NOAH'S ARK

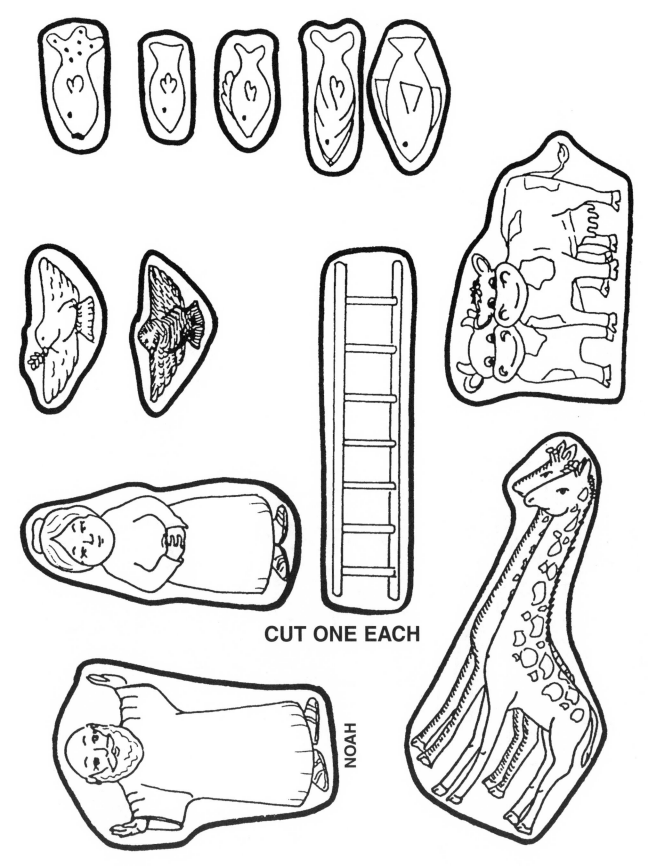

CUT ONE EACH

NOAH

23

NOAH'S ARK

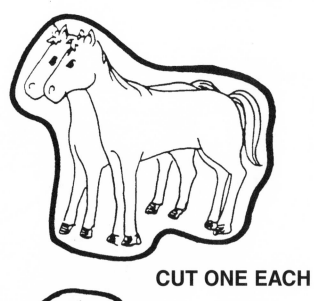

CUT ONE EACH

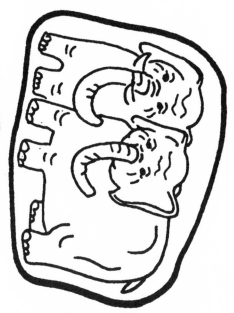

4. MOSES IN THE RUSHES

Based on Exodus 1;2

Materials

Crayons
Markers or Paints
Scissors
Glue/Staples

Time required: 20–25 minutes

Directions

1. Read story and review lesson.
2. Color pieces. Decorate. Cut out. Fold the basket lid closed. Decorate the lid.
3. Place baby Moses in the basket, weaving the feet through the two slots provided. Close the basket lid.
4. Fold the bottom of the band sections **back.**
5. Glue or staple sides. Connect the band (water and reeds) section. Size to fit.
6. Tuck basket into water slot. Place Moses' sister in the slot behind left reed section. (Roll tape to hold her in place if necessary.)

Suggestions

- Add bits of cloth to clothing, scraps of yarn for hair.
- Add toothpicks or bits of straw to the reeds.
- Add glitter or sequins to Pharaoh's daughter's gown.
- Use rolled tape to hold the figures in place for transit.
- Provide an envelope for the pieces.

25

To Make This Craft Special...

★ Talk about the Nile River, its varying depths and its long length. Explain its importance in a land with so much desert area. Talk about the reeds.

★ Sing songs that tell of love and babies, such as "Lullaby and Good Night."

★ Have the children talk about someone who really loves them and wants to do all he or she can do to help them.

★ Have children talk about some difficult decisions their families have made. (i.e., moving from a house to an apartment, grandma and grandpa having to move to a warmer climate so they can have better health, giving away a family pet because it is not the best life for the pet, et cetera)

★ As a group, compose a letter that Moses' mother might have written to explain to Moses why he went to live with someone else.

★ As a group, compose a letter that Miriam might have written to Moses telling him how much she loves him and how much she misses growing up with her brother.

★ If *Moses in the Rushes* is to be used as a hat only, glue the pieces in place so that Pharaoh's daughter is finding the child, Miriam is about to come out of hiding and Moses' mother is off to the side. Glue the edge of the basket only so that Moses can still slip in and out.

Send Home

• Send the story *Moses in the Rushes* home with each child so that the sharing and retelling of the story can continue.

• Roll the story and hold it closed with a heart sticker. The heart represents the love that Moses' mother and sister had for Moses.

MOSES IN THE RUSHES

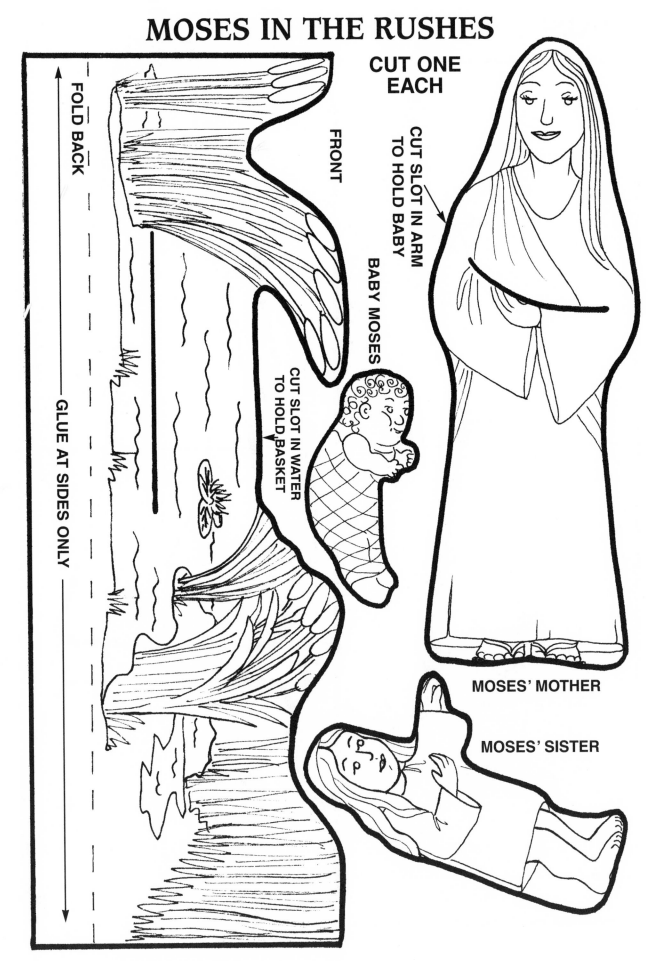

CUT ONE EACH

FRONT

CUT SLOT IN ARM
TO HOLD BABY

BABY MOSES

CUT SLOT IN WATER
TO HOLD BASKET

FOLD BACK

GLUE AT SIDES ONLY

MOSES' MOTHER

MOSES' SISTER

29

MOSES IN THE RUSHES

GLUE

FOLD BACK

FOLD ARMS UP
(TO HOLD MOSES)

SIDES—GLUE TO FRONT—ADJUST AT BACK CUT TWO

PHARAOH'S DAUGHTER

CUT ONE

CUT SLOTS FOR BABY

GLUE

5. CROSSING THE RED SEA

Based on Exodus 14;15

Materials

Crayons
Markers or Paints
Brass Fasteners (2)
Scissors
Glue/Staples
Tape

Time required: 20–30 minutes

Directions

1. Read story and review lesson.
2. Color pieces. Cut out.
3. Fold up front slot section. Color to match the land.
4. Use hole punch to make holes in front section and water sections.
5. Place water sections in slot and insert brass fastener through all three sections (front, water, land). Place tape over the open sharp ends of brass fasteners to secure flat.
6. Cut an envelope to form a small (2 1/2" x 6 1/2" approx.) pocket. Glue to the back of front section to hold pieces and to aid in telling the story.
7. When Moses lifts his staff, the water can be put in the up position. When the soldiers come through, the water closes down on them.

Suggestions

- Glue a small stick to make Moses' staff.
- Dab sand on the land. (Brush on a mixture of glue and water in spots and sprinkle sand on the area.)
- Add blue tissue paper to the water sections.

To Make This Craft Special...

★ While the children are working, play marching songs to get the feel of the Exodus.

★ Use a yardstick to demonstrate how Moses used the staff in the story.

★ Act out parting the sea. Have two children stand a few feet apart facing one another. Have them hold hands at waist level to form a barrier. When the rod (yardstick) is lifted, the children should raise their hands up over their heads similar to "London Bridge," but letting go. Have another child cross through the open space. Next, have another child walk through. Hold out the rod and have the arms come down around them.

★ If *Crossing the Red Sea* is to be used as a hat only, glue Moses to the side. Glue the soldiers and Israelites at opposite sides of the wall of water. Allow the water to still move freely on the brass fasteners.

★ Tape should be placed over the open end of the brass fasteners to hold them firmly against the band. The tape will also protect the child's hair from being pulled and head from being scratched.

Send Home

• Send the story *Crossing the Red Sea* home with each child so that the sharing and retelling of the story can continue.

• Roll the story and hold it closed with a special sticker or a paper loop. If using a loop, put short sides together, overlapping slightly. Tape. Slip the rolled story into the loop. When the child takes the story home, the loop can be torn, releasing the page from its bonds—like the people were released from their bonds.

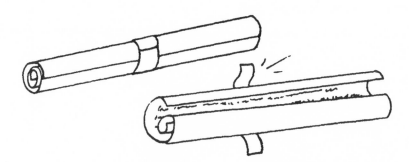

CROSSING THE RED SEA

Based on Exodus 14;15

The Israelites lived in the land of Egypt. Egypt was ruled by a Pharaoh who made the Israelite people work like slaves. God chose Moses to take the Israelites out of Egypt to the Promised Land. The Israelites wanted to leave Egypt and go with Moses.

Moses went to Pharaoh many times and said, "Let my people go!" Each time, Pharaoh said, "No!" He did not want the Israelite people to leave. Pharaoh got angry and made the people work even harder.

Moses called on God. God sent much unhappiness to the land of Egypt. Finally, the Pharaoh got tired of the bad things happening and told Moses, "Rise up, go out of Egypt. Take the Israelites with you!" The Israelites were free!

Soon Moses and the Israelites were leaving Egypt on the long journey across the desert. After a time they came to the Red Sea.

In the meantime Pharaoh started to change his mind. He was sorry that he let the Israelites go. He decided to send an army after the people to make them come back and work for him again.

When the Israelites saw the army coming from behind and saw the sea in front of them, they were frightened. They became angry with Moses. They said, "Why did you bring us here. We will die."

Moses said, "Do not be afraid. The Lord will help us."

Moses prayed to God for help. God told Moses to stretch a rod over the sea to open the sea. Moses held his staff out over the water. The sea parted! The Israelites walked safely to the opposite side over a dry path between the high walls of water. The Egyptian soldiers saw this and hurried after the people along the same path. When the Pharaoh's army reached the center, God told Moses to stretch a rod over the water again. The two walls of water rolled back over the path. The Pharaoh's army was buried in the sea. The Israelites were safe on the other side.

Moses and God's people sang songs of happy praise to God!

LESSON PLAN

Objectives:

1. To see that God loved the Israelites and helped them to flee Egypt.
2. To see that we, too, can call on God in time of need.
3. To show God's power.
4. To develop the concept of "miracle."
5. To show that enslavement is wrong.
6. To follow general and specific directions.
7. To _____.

Theme: God loves and watches over us all. We can call on him in time of need.

Preparation:

In this story you will learn about Moses and the Israelites. You will also hear about a pharaoh. A pharaoh is like a king. Let's see how God helped the people.

Read the story *Crossing the Red Sea.*

Discuss/Ask:

Why was Moses trying to get Pharaoh to let the people go? How would you have felt if you had to work like a slave for the Pharaoh? Did Pharaoh want the Israelite people to go out of Egypt? Why not? What made him finally let the people go? The people were happy at first to follow Moses, but what happened to make them afraid? How did God help the Israelites when the army started to come after them? What did this miracle show the people?

Explain:

God showed the people his love and his power. When Moses called upon God for the people, he listened. God could control the seas because he has power over all things. God was guiding the people and they needed to put their trust in him. Likewise, we can trust in God. We should not let bad habits enslave us. We should pray and ask God for his help in our lives.

Follow Directions for Craft.

CROSSING THE RED SEA

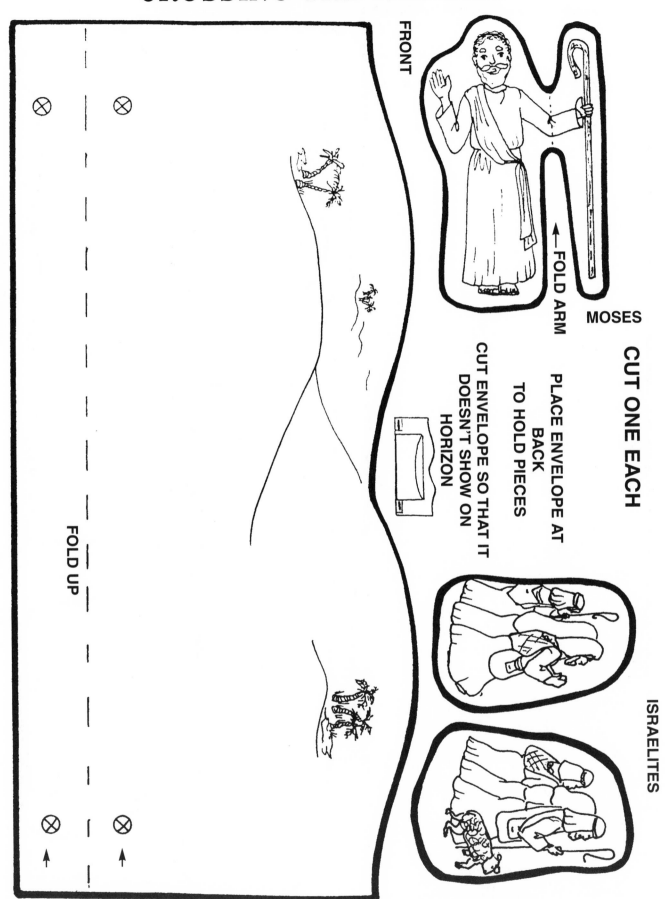

FRONT

MOSES

FOLD ARM

CUT ONE EACH

PLACE ENVELOPE AT
BACK
TO HOLD PIECES

CUT ENVELOPE SO THAT IT
DOESN'T SHOW ON
HORIZON

FOLD UP

ISRAELITES

HOLE PUNCH. INSERT BRASS FASTENERS

35

CROSSING THE RED SEA

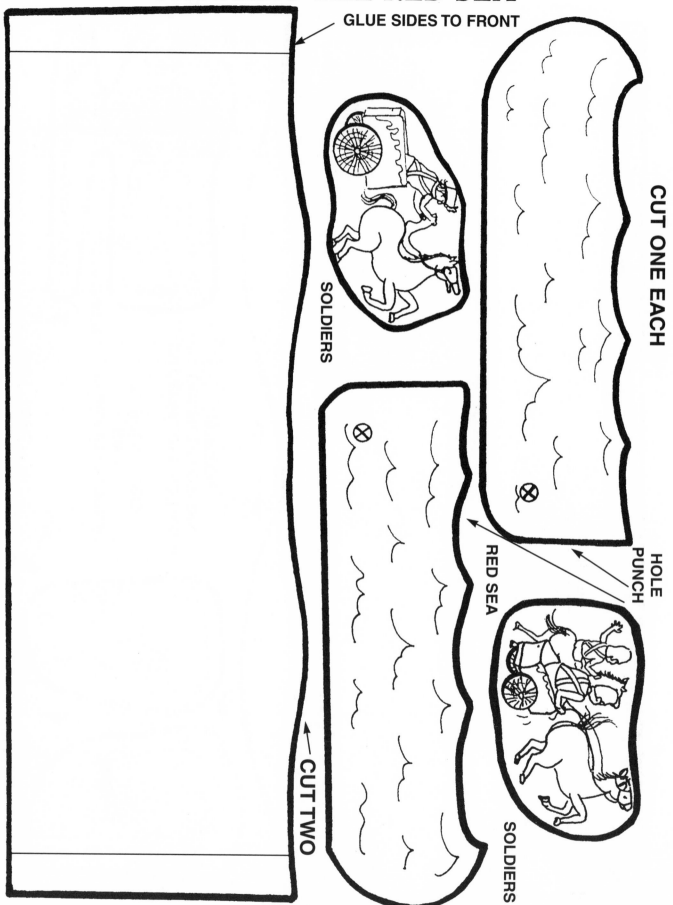

GLUE SIDES TO FRONT

CUT ONE EACH

SOLDIERS

HOLE PUNCH

RED SEA

CUT TWO

SOLDIERS

36

6. THE TEN COMMANDMENTS

Based on Exodus 19;20;30;31

Materials

Tissue Paper
Crayons
Markers or Paints
Scissors
Glue/Staples

Time required: 20–25 minutes

Directions

1. Read story and review lesson.
2. Color and cut all pieces.
3. Fold up the front bottom section to form a stand for the people. Glue thin sides only.
4. Attach sides to front.
5. Glue or staple at back; adjust to fit.
6. Glue tissue paper "lightning" in place.

Suggestions

- Add scraps of cloth to clothing and yarn for a belt.
- Add tiny rocks as "boulders" to the front folded-up section of the hat.
- Have the children collect small bits of real greenery for shrubs. Glue to mountain or glue to the front fold.
- Moisten and seal an envelope. Cut it in half down the middle to form two pockets. Glue a pocket to the back of the mountain (just below the "lightning") to hold Moses when he goes to the top of the mountain, to hold the tablets before he receives them, and later, to hold the pieces to be transported home.

To Make This Craft Special...

★ Make "thunder" sounds by shaking aluminum foil or rolling a pencil over an empty paper towel tube. Also, "God's great voice" can be made by speaking into the paper towel tube. When God speaks, the "lightning" can rise from the mountain.

★ If *The Ten Commandments* is to be used as a hat only, glue the pieces in place. Roll tape (or glue) the tablets in Moses' arms. Roll tape to hold Moses in place as he is coming down the mountain.

★ While the children are working, play songs that express God's love.

★ Make a chart with the numbers 1 to 3 on one side and 4 to 10 on the other. Have the children help to write the ten commandments, giving examples of putting them into practice in their lives.

Send Home

• Send the story *The Ten Commandments* home with each child so that the sharing and retelling of the story can continue.

• The bottom portion of the commandments can be cut out and glued to a tablet-shaped piece of paper or cardboard.

• Roll the story like a scroll and send it home sealed with a sticker that expresses the theme of God's love, or fold the story and put it in the envelope already glued to the inside band.

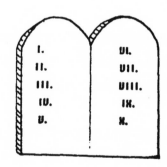

THE TEN COMMANDMENTS

Based on Exodus 19;20;30;31

Moses and the Israelites marched across the desert. It was not an easy trip. But God watched over the people. God sent them food from heaven, birds to eat and water to drink. Still, they often complained.

After three long months they came to a place called Mount Sinai. They set up camp there. Moses went up into the mountain to talk to God. God made a promise: The Israelites were a special people, but they must obey God. Moses came down the mountain and told the people of God's promise.

Later Moses went up into the mountain to talk to God again. The people stayed at the bottom of the mountain. They could hear thunder and see lightning. They could hear God's booming voice, but could not understand God's words. Moses came back to the people saying, " We must obey God's laws." The people said, "Yes, we will obey."

Again God called Moses to come up into the mountain. This time God wrote the laws down for the people on two large stone slabs. Moses was up on the mountain for forty days and forty nights. While he was gone, the people forgot their promise to God. The people began to do bad things. Moses came down the mountain and saw the people praising a golden statue. He became angry. Moses threw the stone slabs down, smashing them. Still, God was good. Once more, Moses went up into the mountain to talk to the Lord. God wrote the commandments again on two new slabs. Moses returned to the people and gave them the commandments. They were for all people.

The Ten Commandments:

I.	I am the Lord your God	VI.	Do not commit adultery
II.	Keep holy the Lord's name	VII.	Do not steal
III.	Keep holy the Lord's day	VIII.	Do not lie
IV.	Honor your father and mother	IX.	Do not desire your neighbor's wife.
V.	Do not kill	X.	Do not desire your neighbor's goods.

LESSON PLAN

Objectives:

1. To show God's love and promise for us.
2. To show how Moses shepherded the Israelites across the desert.
3. To develop an understanding of how hard it is at times to have faith.
4. To show the importance of faith.
5. To learn the ten commandments, God's rules for us.
6. To _____.

Theme: Have faith in God. He loves us and watches over us. God has given us commandments by which to live.

Preparation:

The Israelites left a land where they had been treated poorly, but still they were not very happy. If you had to travel through a strange land to get to a new home, you might be confused too, especially if it took a long time. This story tells us about the Israelites and Moses in the desert and how God was watching out for them.

Read the story *The Ten Commandments*.

Discuss/Ask:

Why do you think the people were confused? God understood that the people needed a lot of guidance. Why do you think God didn't make it easier for the people? (He was showing them that they needed to have faith.) He chose Moses to watch over them partly because of Moses' own great faith. When it was time to explain to the people how they should act, God chose to speak to Moses. God tested the Israelites' faith, but he also wrote down laws for them so that they would know how they were to live their lives. How are these laws for us today?

Explain:

God gave the Ten Commandments to Moses a long time ago, but the commandments are still to be obeyed today. They are guides that God has given to us. The Ten Commandments show God's love and promise for us all.

Follow Directions for Craft.

THE TEN COMMANDMENTS

GLUE TO SIDES
OF FRONT HERE

ISRAELITES

CUT TWO

FOLD

MOSES

FOLD

CUT
ONE
EACH

FOLD ARMS AT LINES
TO HOLD TABLETS

SIDES

CUT ONE →

I   VI
II   VII
III   VIII
IV   IX
V   X

← ADJUST TO FIT

THE TABLETS

THE TEN COMMANDMENTS

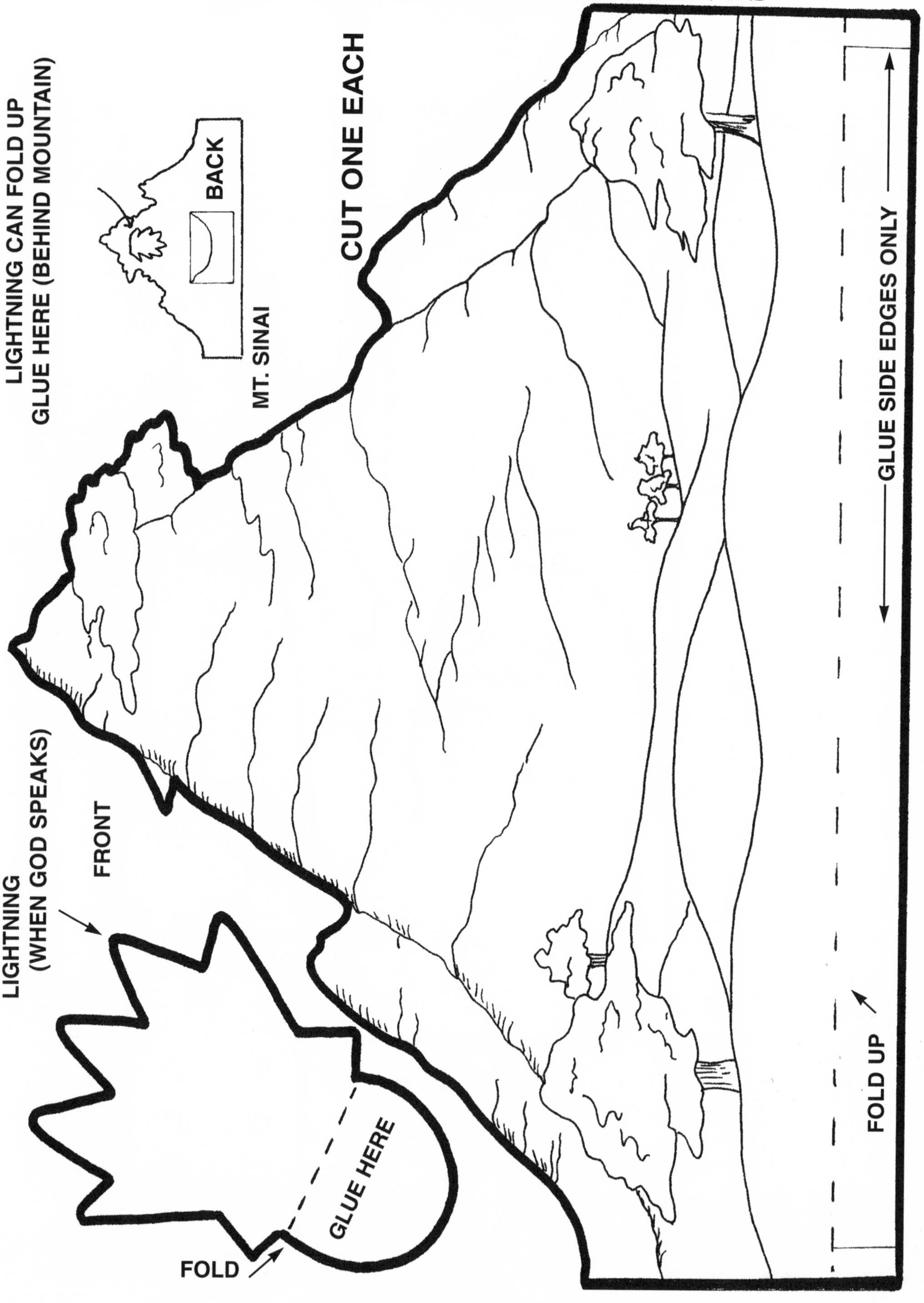

CUT ONE EACH

LIGHTNING CAN FOLD UP
GLUE HERE (BEHIND MOUNTAIN)

BACK

MT. SINAI

GLUE SIDE EDGES ONLY

LIGHTNING
(WHEN GOD SPEAKS)

FRONT

GLUE HERE

FOLD

FOLD UP

42

7. JONAH AND THE WHALE

Based on the Book of Jonah

Materials

Crayons
Markers
Scissors
Glue
Brass Fastener

Time required: 25–30 minutes

Directions

1. Read story and review lesson.
2. Color pieces. Cut out. Carefully cut wave slots and land slot.
3. Connect land and water pieces to form headband. Size to fit.
4. Glue outside **edges only** of boat so that Jonah can fit into the "pocket" formed.
5. Fold bottom of whale back on dotted line. Glue or staple the small front edge of mouth *only*. Put the whale's head into the slot formed and push a brass fastener through all three pieces as shown. (Mouth should open and close. Jonah should fit into the slot.)
6. Add tree to land area.

Suggestions

- Glue tiny shells to the land or in the water.
- Draw or glue tiny pictures of fish to the water.
- Add thin ribbon strips to the head of the whale to resemble water spouting.
- Add tiny scraps of fabric to Jonah to make clothes.
- Add bits of yarn for hair.
- Add a button or sequin eye to the whale.

To Make This Craft Special...

★ Place a large blanket in the middle of the room. Have each child climb under it and ask them to imagine that they are in the belly of a whale.

★ Children can act out the story, taking different parts. The floor is the "land," the carpet area is the "water," a cardboard box is the "boat" and the blanket is the "whale."

★ If *Jonah and the Whale* is to be used as a hat only, glue the pieces in place. Allow for the mouth to open and close. Put Jonah in the whale's mouth.

★ Play songs about whales, fish and the sea. Play "nature sounds" of the sea while the children are working.

Send Home

● Send the story *Jonah and the Whale* home with each child so that the sharing and retelling of the story can continue.

● Fold the story like a boat (fig. 1, a and b); or roll and secure with a sticker that has a sea or fish motif (fig. 2).

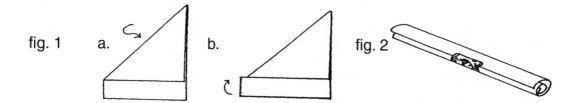

JONAH AND THE WHALE

Based on the Book of Jonah

God spoke to a man named Jonah. God said, "Nineveh, the great city, is wicked. Go to Nineveh and preach to the people. Tell them to behave."

At the command, Jonah got up, but he did not obey. Jonah planned to run away from the Lord. He went to the town of Joppa and found a ship going to Tarshish. Jonah thought he had tricked God by hiding. When the ship was out at sea, God sent a violent storm. The sailors on the boat were afraid. Meanwhile, Jonah was fast asleep in the bottom of the boat. The captain came to Jonah, shook him saying, "Get up! Call upon your God for help."

The storm continued. The sailors decided to cast lots (a kind of dice game) to find out who was making God angry. The lot fell upon Jonah. Jonah admitted that he had been running away from the Lord. He knew that God had sent the storm because he had not obeyed. Then Jonah told the men to throw him into the sea. The men did not know what to do. They rowed harder and harder to get to the land, but the storm just got worse. Finally, they did throw Jonah into the sea. The waters became calm. The men on the ship prayed, "Forgive us, Lord, for throwing Jonah into the sea."

In the meantime, the Lord sent a large fish—a whale! The whale scooped Jonah out of the water and swallowed him. He remained in the belly of the whale three days and three nights. From inside the whale, Jonah prayed to the Lord. He promised to obey God. After the third day, the Lord commanded the whale to throw Jonah onto the dry land.

This time Jonah got up and went straight to Nineveh! Jonah told the people that God was going to destroy the city in forty days. The people listened. Everyone in the city, even the king, began to fast and change their ways. Nineveh was spared.

God is loving and merciful!

LESSON PLAN

Objectives:

1. To show that God never stops loving us.
2. To see how everyone makes mistakes and we can be forgiven.
3. To begin to understand God's mercy.
4. To follow general and specific directions.
5. To _____.
6. (Older children.) To see how the number *three* is used to foreshadow the resurrection.

Theme: God never stops loving us.

Preparation:

Did you ever try to run away from a problem? Why? What happened? Usually when we try to run away from a problem, it doesn't go away. Sometimes it even gets worse. In this story, God guides a man back to him in a very special way.

Read the story *Jonah and the Whale.*

Discuss/Ask:

Why did Jonah run away? Do you think it is a little bit funny that he thought he could hide from God? How do you think Jonah felt when God put him in the belly of the whale? When was he set free? Why do you think God used a whale in this story?

Sometimes God might ask you to do something you don't want to do. Do you think that hiding would be the best way to handle the situation? Why or why not? Even if we do make mistakes and turn away, God will always love us. He will lead us back. Why should we trust in God's love? (It is endless.)

Explain:

God loves us and sees all that we do. His love will always be there for us. (Older children: In this Old Testament story Jonah is in the belly of the whale for three days. It is almost as if he is dead to the world for that time. Then he is returned unharmed to the shore. What event in the New Testament is this foreshadowing? The resurrection.)

Follow Directions for Craft.

JONAH AND THE WHALE

JONAH

CUT ONE EACH

WHALE

HOLE
PUNCH
FOR
BRASS
FASTENER

47

JONAH AND THE WHALE

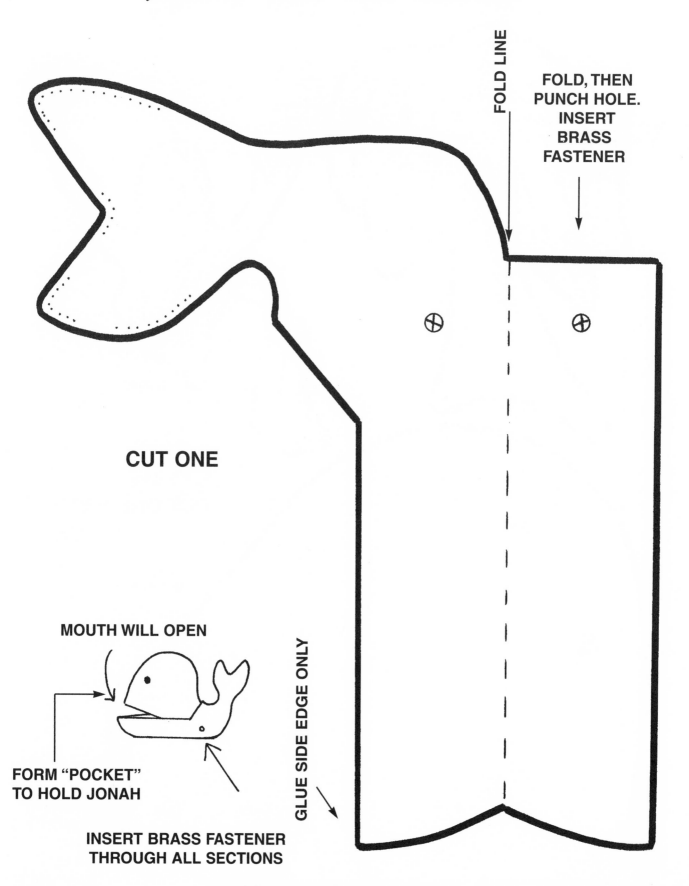

FOLD LINE

FOLD, THEN
PUNCH HOLE.
INSERT
BRASS
FASTENER

CUT ONE

MOUTH WILL OPEN

GLUE SIDE EDGE ONLY

FORM "POCKET"
TO HOLD JONAH

INSERT BRASS FASTENER
THROUGH ALL SECTIONS

48

JONAH AND THE WHALE

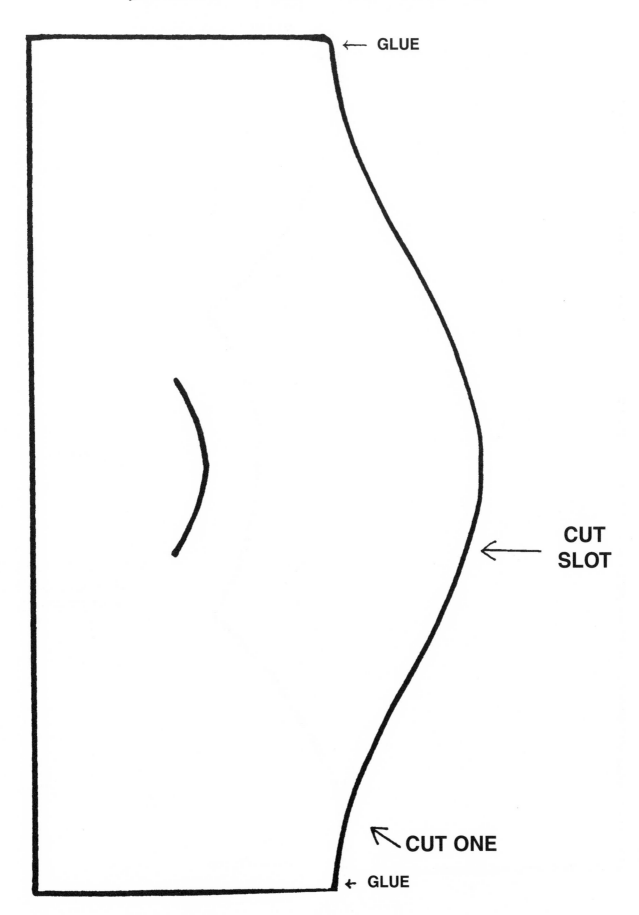

GLUE

CUT
SLOT

CUT ONE

GLUE

JONAH AND THE WHALE

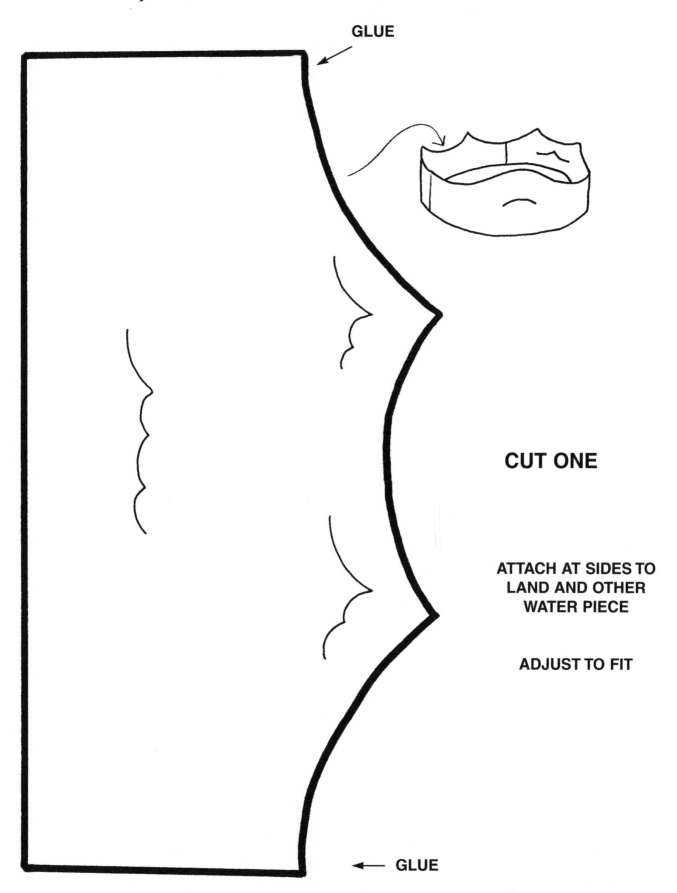

GLUE

CUT ONE

ATTACH AT SIDES TO
LAND AND OTHER
WATER PIECE

ADJUST TO FIT

← GLUE

JONAH AND THE WHALE

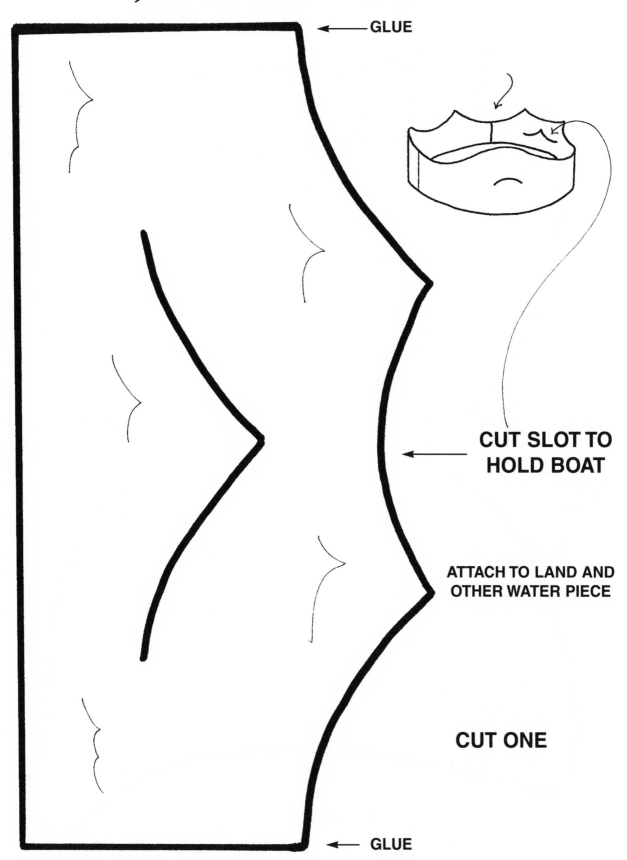

GLUE

GLUE

CUT SLOT TO
HOLD BOAT

ATTACH TO LAND AND
OTHER WATER PIECE

CUT ONE

JONAH AND THE WHALE

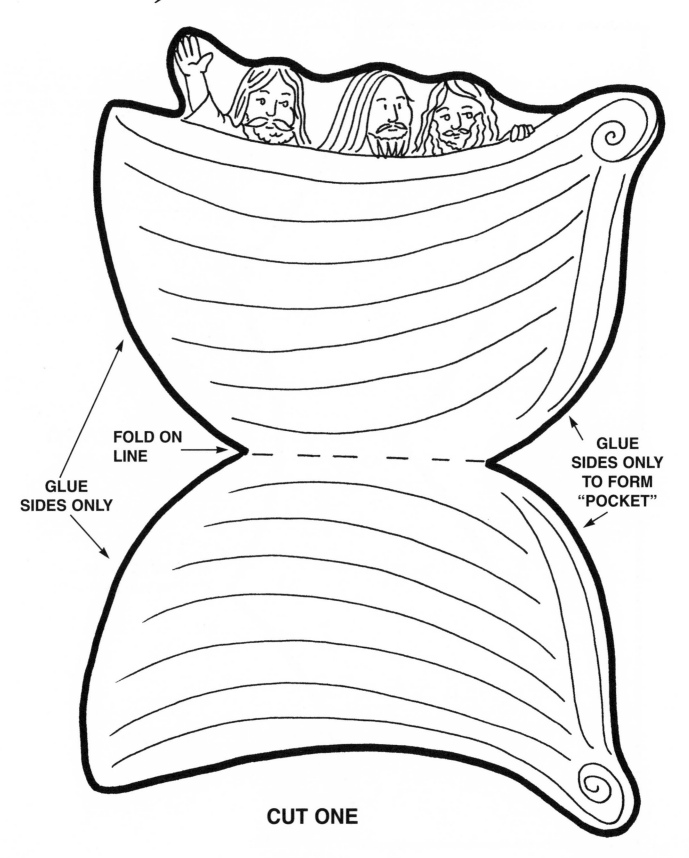

GLUE
SIDES ONLY

FOLD ON
LINE

GLUE
SIDES ONLY
TO FORM
"POCKET"

CUT ONE

8. DAVID AND GOLIATH

Based on 1 Samuel 17:41-50

Materials

Crayons
Markers or Paints
Small stone
Scissors
Glue
Staples

Time required: 30–35 minutes

Directions

1. Read story and review lesson.
2. Color and cut all pieces. Cut the rock and mound at dark lines. David can stand behind the rock. When Goliath is slain, he is turned over and the "mound" will hold his body. (Tuck inside.)
3. Connect hat fronts together at center.
4. Glue or staple back of hat at sides, adjusting to fit.
5. Fold sling line for David so that he can hurl stone.

Suggestions

- Add tiny pebbles to the ground area.
- Draw arrows on the hill of the battlefield.
- Add bits of cloth to David and Goliath.
- Add glitter to the spears and shields.
- Add foil scraps to Goliath's shield.
- Add a bright small scrap of red tissue to the wound made by David's stone.
- Draw more soldiers in the ranks.

To Make This Craft Special...

★ Show pictures of David and Goliath from other Bible story manuals to see how different artists have illustrated the scene.

★ Discuss the weapons, et cetera, used in the time of David. (such as shields, lances, spears, bows and arrows...). Then show five small shiny stones. Stress that with faith, a small stone was enough for David to win against Goliath.

★ Read some of the psalms attributed to David's authorship to show his strong relationship with God.

★ If *David and Goliath* is to be used as a hat only, glue David in place. Tape Goliath so that he can still be used in a standing or fallen position.

Send Home

• Send the story *David and Goliath* home with each child so that the sharing and retelling of the story can continue.

• Roll the story and send it home tied with a piece of leather fringe or abaca-type cord or yarn to suggest David's sling shot material.

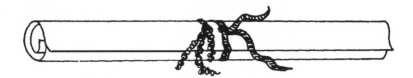

DAVID AND GOLIATH

Based on 1 Samuel 17:1-50

David was a young shepherd boy. He was the youngest of many brothers. Now and then David would leave his father's home and come to the battlefield because his brothers were fighting there. Sometimes he would take them food and drink. David also helped King Saul.

King Saul and his army were fighting the Philistines.

The Philistines had a soldier in their army who was big and mighty. His name was Goliath. Goliath bragged about his strength and teased Saul's army. Several times he called to Saul's army, trying to get them to send a man to fight with him. David was taking food to his brothers when he heard the mighty Goliath call, "Give me a man so I can fight him!"

David went to King Saul and said, "Let me go and fight the mighty Philistine!" The king did not want David to fight Goliath. David was a boy and Goliath was a giant of a man. He had been a warrior for many years.

David told the king that he had fought many animals, keeping them away from the sheep. He could fight a big bear of a man like Goliath too. "And," David said, "the Lord will save me from the hand of this Philistine." Saul agreed and said, "Go, and may the Lord be with you!"

David prepared for battle, but he could not wear the armor the king gave him. It was too heavy. He would fight Goliath without armor.

David got his sling and five smooth stones.

Goliath was protected with armor and a shield. He saw David coming and teased him for being small. The giant Philistine moved toward David. David moved toward the Philistine. They called to each other.

David took a stone from his bag and put it in the sling. He hurled it at Goliath. The stone struck the Philistine on the forehead. Goliath fell to the ground.

Saul's army was glad! They began to cheer. David had beaten Goliath. Later, David would become the king. God had blessed him.

God gives us courage and strength!

LESSON PLAN

Objectives:

1. To show that "might does not make right."
2. To develop an awareness of goodness winning out over evil.
3. To develop an understanding of the power of faith, the importance of trust.
4. To show how God loves and protects us all.
5. To follow general and specific directions.
6. To _____.

Theme: Faith and trust in God can help us overcome great odds.

Preparation:

Let's pretend a coin fell down into a hole. The hole was small and not very deep. A large hand could not fit into the hole to get the coin, but a small one could. Would you ask your big brother, big sister or someone with a large hand to try to get the coin? Would you use **your** smaller hand to get the coin out? What if a ball rolled behind a big bush that only had a small crawl space behind it. Who could reach it better, someone big or someone small? Sometimes large is not better.

Read the story *David and Goliath.*

Discuss/Ask:

Goliath was big and very strong. He could wear the heavy armor. David was small, but smart and fast on his feet. He could use his sling well. Best of all he had a special weapon. Do you know what it was? (Faith in God.) This faith was the special help David needed. Quote the response: "David said he trusted that the Lord God would be with him in the battle."
How do you think David felt when he realized he won the battle? How do you think King Saul felt? How do you think the great army behind Goliath felt when they saw him fall? Would David have gone up against Goliath if he didn't have faith in God?

Explain:

There were differences between David and Goliath such as size, strength, experience, and so forth. Still, God loved and protected David. We, too, should have faith and trust in God.

Follow Directions for Craft.

DAVID AND GOLIATH

FOLD, GLUE TOGETHER

CUT ONE

FOLD

GOLIATH

57

DAVID AND GOLIATH

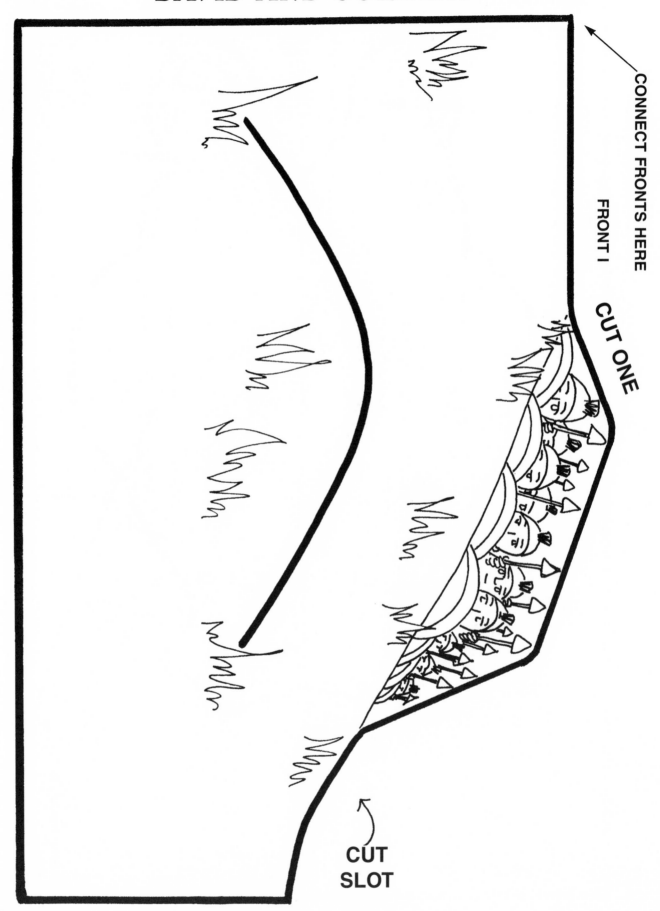

CONNECT FRONTS HERE

FRONT I

CUT ONE

CUT SLOT

58

DAVID AND GOLIATH

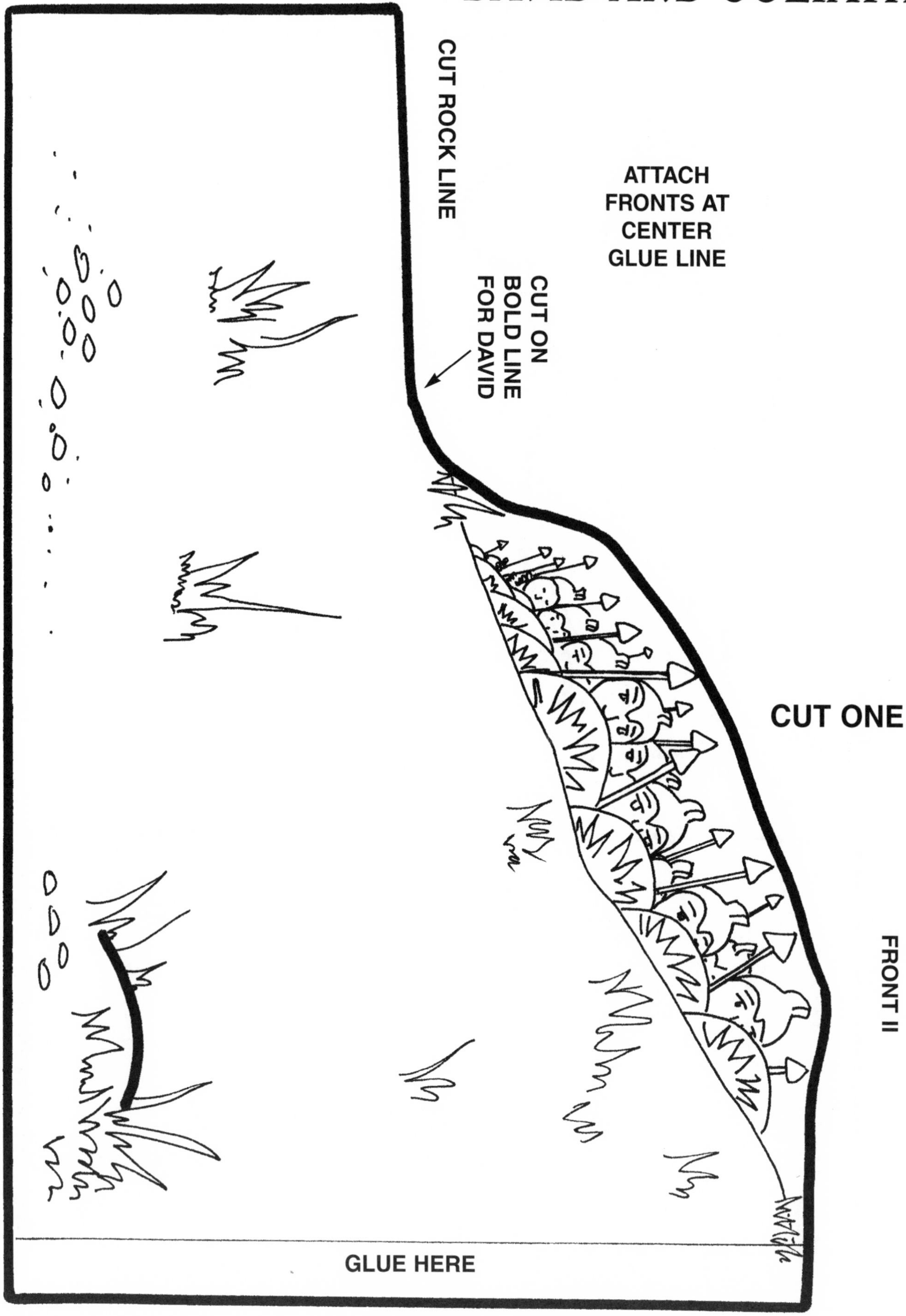

CUT ROCK LINE

ATTACH
FRONTS AT
CENTER
GLUE LINE

CUT ON
BOLD LINE
FOR DAVID

CUT ONE

FRONT II

GLUE HERE

59

DAVID AND GOLIATH

FOLD LINE

SLING WILL MOVE FORWARD

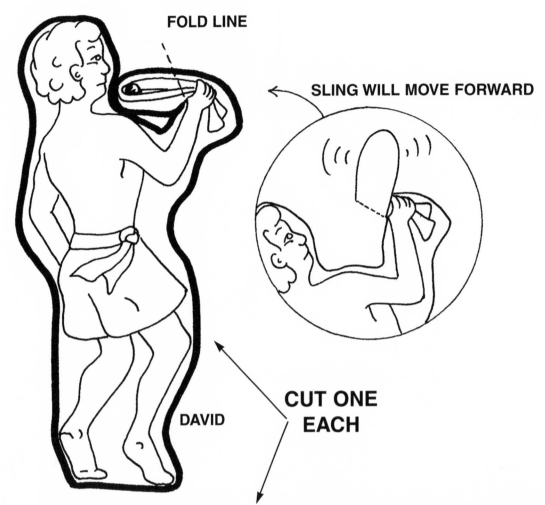

CUT ONE
EACH

DAVID

BACK   USE THIS PIECE TO ADJUST THE HAT TO FIT

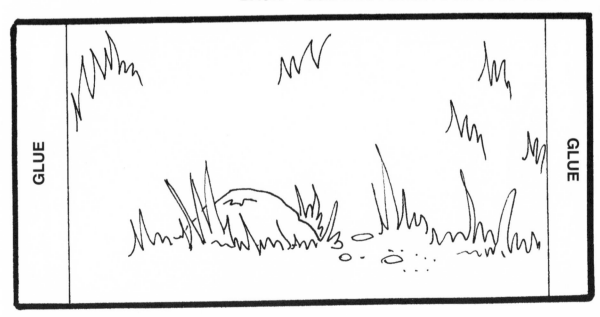

GLUE   GLUE

9. THE NATIVITY

Based on Luke 2:1-20

Materials

Crayons
Markers or Paints
Scissors
Glue
Thread/String

Time required: 25–30 minutes

Directions

1. Read story and review lesson.
2. Color or paint pieces. Cut out. Carefully cut all dark-lined slots.
3. Fold front of stable up and glue or staple side edges **only.**
4. Add sides to headband. Adjust to fit at back.
5. Place Mary and Joseph into appropriate slots. (Tuck Mary's and Joseph's heads under roof line slots.) Slide Jesus into the manger, weaving in and out.
6. Attach star to roof.
7. Tape a piece of thread to the back of the angel (angel will appear to fly over stable) or roll a piece of tape and attach angel to roof.

Suggestions

- Add bits of straw to the hay.
- Glitter Jesus' halo and the star.
- Add scraps of cloth to clothing.
- Draw animals in the stable.
- Add small feathers to the angel's wings.

To Make This Craft Special...

★ Play Christmas carols while the children are working.

★ Explain and illustrate the term "swaddling clothes." These are long thin strips of cloth, still used today in many countries, that hold a baby's body and feet snugly in place. Babies are sometimes wrapped this way when they are to ride on the mother's back while she is working. Demonstrate with a doll and a cloth wrap (like those used to wrap a knee or ankle) or make "swaddling clothes" by using paper towels. Allow 4 or 5 towels to remain attached; cut down the middle to form long strips. Hold the end of the towel at the feet and wrap up to the stomach.

★ A small picture of a child dressed in a paper doll costume can be placed with the shepherds as if the child were there on the first Christmas.

★ If *The Nativity* is to be used as a hat only, glue the pieces in place. Place shepherds to the side. If the optional wise men are used, glue them to the opposite side. The angel can be glued to roof edge or be unattached.

Send Home

• Send the story *The Nativity* home with each child so that the sharing and retelling can continue.

• Roll the story like a scroll. Use a thin piece of bedsheet cloth as a tie to hold the roll making reference to "swaddling clothes." Or, send the scroll home secured with an angel sticker.

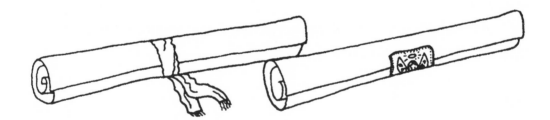

THE NATIVITY
Based on Luke 2:1-20

Caesar Augustus ordered all of the people in the land to go to the homes of their births and be counted. So Joseph went from the town of Nazareth to the far away city of Bethlehem. He went with Mary, his wife, who was going to have a baby very soon. When they arrived in Bethlehem, there was no room for them in the inn, the place where travelers stayed. They found shelter where the animals were kept. While they were there, Mary gave birth to the baby named Jesus. She wrapped fresh strips of cloth ("swaddling clothes") around the baby and used a manger for a bed. How happy they were!

There were shepherds nearby that lived in the fields. They were watching over their sheep during the night. The Lord's angel came to them. They were very frightened. The angel told them: "Do not be afraid. You should be happy! I come to tell you good news—joyous news! This good news is for all people. A savior has been born in Bethlehem. This child is the Messiah (Savior). You will see the child wrapped in bands of cloth and lying in a manger."

Suddenly, many more angels appeared. They were singing, "Glory to God in the highest heaven. Peace to all the people of the earth!"

After the angels left, the shepherds began to talk about what they had just seen. They decided to go to Bethlehem to find the child. They hurried to Bethlehem and found Mary and Joseph with the baby. The baby Jesus was lying in the manger. When they saw the baby, they understood what the angel had said. Jesus was indeed special!

Later, the shepherds returned home and told everyone what they had heard and seen.

Glory to God in high heaven!

LESSON PLAN

Objectives:

1. To develop an appreciation for God's love by focusing on the fulfillment of his promise to send a savior.
2. To understand the importance of family.
3. To understand love and commitment.
4. To begin to develop a sense of awe and praise for the miracle birth of Jesus.
5. To understand Mary and Joseph's obedience to God.
6. To follow general and specific directions.
7. To _____.

Theme: God shows his love by sending his son to earth as the savior of the world. The holy family is an example of love.

Preparation:

Talk about families. Ask about newborn babies some of the children may have in their families. Did you have a place ready for the new baby (i.e., crib, baby room, et cetera)? What are some of the things you did to get ready for the baby (i.e., prepare room, purchase diapers, crib, stroller, et cetera)? What if the baby arrived when mother was away from home or on a vacation? Today we could drive to a hospital or fly home after the birth. When Jesus was born his family was in a town far from home.

Read the story *The Nativity.*

Discuss/Ask:

When Jesus was born, Mary and Joseph were far from home and there was no room for them in the inn (motel). Mary and Joseph were loving parents. They had always obeyed God and knew he would provide for them. They went to the stable where the animals lived. Explain "manger." How did they use the manger? There weren't any newspapers in those days, no telephones or computers. But, the news of the special birth was told to others. How? (Angels.) What did the angels say that shows all the world should be happy because of Jesus' birth?

Explain:

Today, every Christmas, we celebrate the birth of Jesus. It is a very happy time. God showed his love by sending his son to earth.

Follow Directions for Craft.

THE NATIVITY

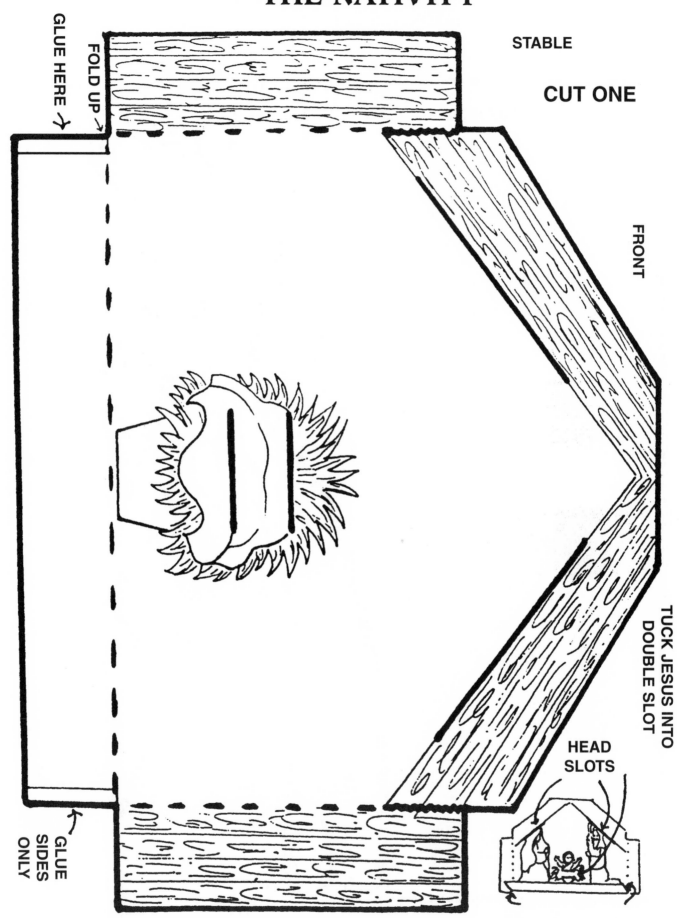

STABLE

CUT ONE

GLUE HERE →

FOLD UP

FRONT

TUCK JESUS INTO DOUBLE SLOT

HEAD SLOTS

GLUE SIDES ONLY

65

THE NATIVITY

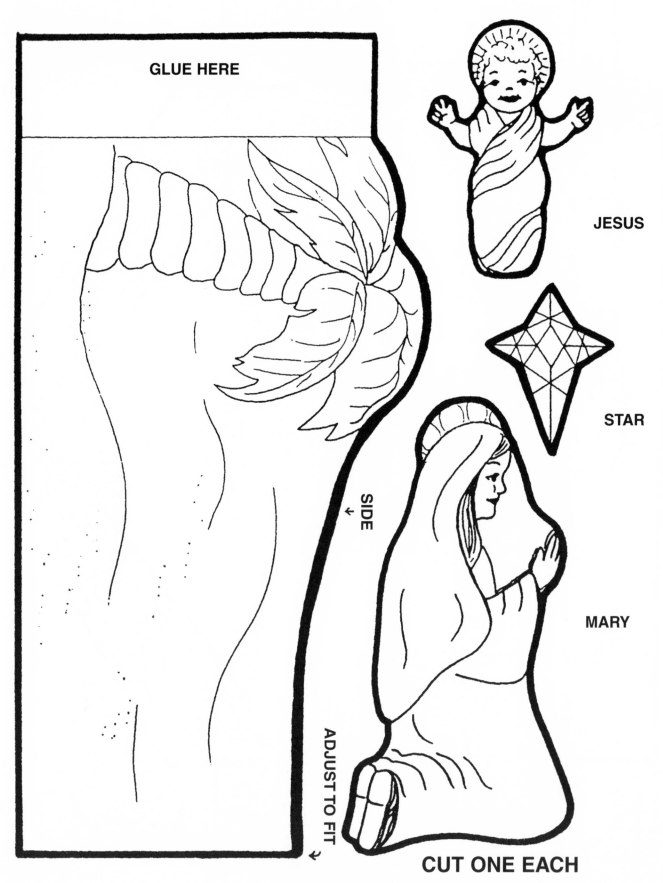

GLUE HERE

SIDE

ADJUST TO FIT

JESUS

STAR

MARY

CUT ONE EACH

THE NATIVITY

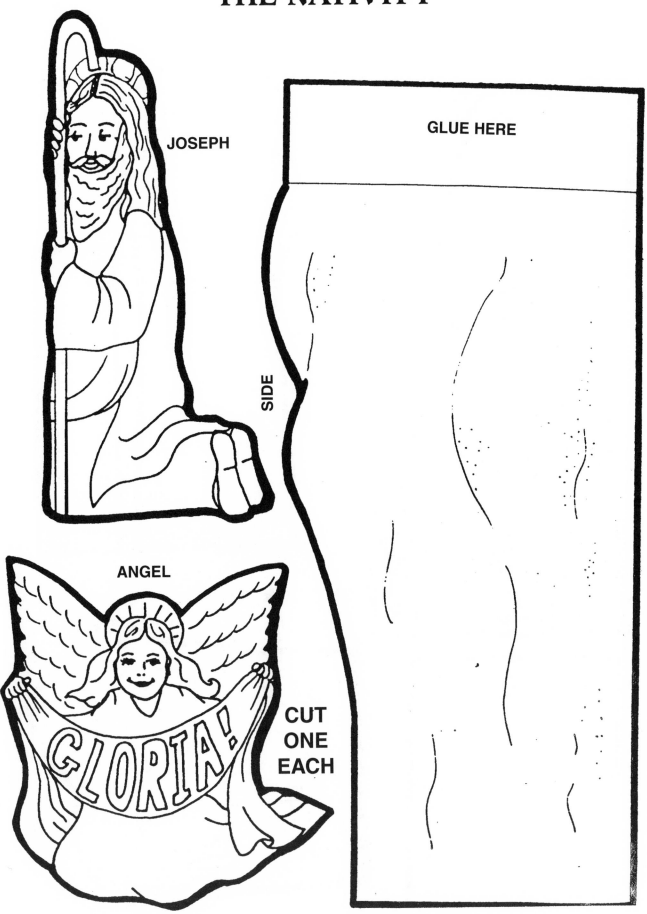

JOSEPH

GLUE HERE

SIDE

ANGEL

GLORIA!

CUT
ONE
EACH

THE NATIVITY

SHEPHERDS

CUT ONE EACH

OPTIONAL STANDS—GLUE TO BACK

FOLD

FOLD

SHEEP

68

THE THREE WISE MEN (OPTIONAL READING)

Matthew 2:1-15

Three wise men came into Jerusalem. They studied the stars and knew that Jesus had been born. A great star had brought them to the city. The wise men were searching for the newborn king of the Jews. They asked, "Where is the child who has been born king of the Jews? We want to praise the newborn king."

Herod, the king, learned that the wise men were asking about a child that would someday lead the people. He learned that Jesus had been born in Bethlehem. Herod met with the wise men. He sent the wise men to look for Jesus. Herod told the wise men, "After you find the child, come and tell me so that I can praise him too."

And they did find Jesus! The star led them on their way and they found Jesus with Mary. How happy they were!

Upon seeing the child, the wise men knew He was the Messiah (chosen one). They knelt and adored the infant king and offered gifts of gold, frankincense and myrrh.

The wise men learned that King Herod was a bad man, so they went back home another way. They did not tell King Herod where Jesus was. But in their own lands they told others about the child Jesus.

Share the Joy, Jesus the savior is born.

THE THREE WISE MEN

THE MAGI

GLUE

GLUE

← STAND ↗

GLUE STAND TO BACK

CUT ONE EACH

10. JESUS IN THE TEMPLE

Based on Luke 2:41-52

Materials

Crayons or Paints
Scissors
Glue or Staples

Time required: 20–25 minutes

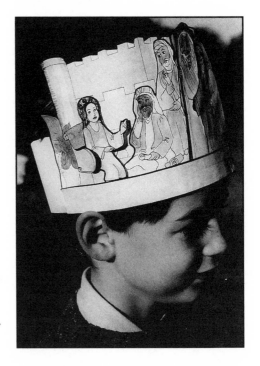

Directions

1. Read story and review lesson.
2. Color or paint pieces. Cut out.
3. Carefully cut on the bold line at the arm section of the chair on the temple scene.
4. Fold up front of temple piece on fold lines; glue together at sides.
5. Glue or staple sides to front, adjusting at back of hat to fit.
6. Fit pieces into slots as marked. Jesus will "sit" in the chair, using the slot cut at the arm section.

Suggestions

- Add scraps of cloth to clothing.
- Add tissue paper scraps to the leaves of the trees.
- Make yarn belts.
- Add a stick to make a staff for Joseph.
- Glitter halos.

To Make This Craft Special...

★ Have three or four shoe box bottoms turned over on a table. Hide something small like a bag of individually wrapped candies, a card of special stickers, et cetera, under one of the boxes. Tell the children that something is hidden under one of the boxes. Have them guess which one. Reveal one of the empty ones, then another empty one. Finally, reveal where the "treasure" is hidden. Ask the children how they felt when they found the "treasure." Remind them how they felt when the first two boxes were turned over. This is, in a very small way, how Mary and Joseph felt. They knew Jesus was probably in Jerusalem somewhere, but they had to keep looking. They were happy when they looked in the right place.

★ Play songs of joy and gladness.

★ If *Jesus in the Temple* is to be used as a hat only, roll tape to keep Jesus in the chair. Roll tape to hold Mary and Joseph to the side, as if they are just coming into the temple.

Send Home

• Send the story *Jesus in the Temple* home with each child so that the sharing and retelling can continue.

• Glue an envelope to the inside back of the temple piece. Fold the story small enough to fit into the envelope. When the story is taken home, the child can play a game of "hide and seek" to preface the storytelling at home. They can ask a parent or brother or sister, "The story of *Jesus in the Temple* is hiding somewhere. Where do you think it is?" The envelope can also serve to hold any pieces for transit.

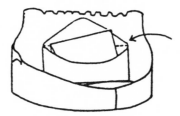

JESUS IN THE TEMPLE
Based on Luke 2:41-52

When Jesus was a boy, Jewish families traveled to the temple in Jerusalem every year during the special season of Passover. When Jesus was twelve years old, Mary and Joseph went to Jerusalem—and this time he went with them.

When the feast was over, Joseph and Mary, with many friends and relatives, started back to their home in Nazareth. They did not realize that Jesus had stayed behind in Jerusalem. Mary thought Jesus was with Joseph; Joseph thought Jesus was with Mary. After a full day's journey, they learned that Jesus was not with them. They were very worried and upset. Mary and Joseph hurried back to the city of Jerusalem.

For two days, Mary and Joseph searched the city for their lost child. Then, on the third day, they went to the temple. There they saw him sitting and talking with the teachers. All who heard Jesus were surprised by his intelligence and wonderful answers.

Seeing him, Mary and Joseph were overjoyed. Still they could not understand why he had stayed behind.

Mary lovingly ran to hug Jesus. Since they had been so sad, she asked Him, "Son, why have you frightened us? We have been looking for you all over Jerusalem."

He replied, "Why did you look for me? Don't you know that I must be in my Father's house?" (Jesus was talking about his Father in heaven.)

Mary and Joseph were confused. Jesus went back to Nazareth with his parents. He grew up there, loving and obeying Mary and Joseph. Mary thought about what Jesus had said and kept his words in her heart.

LESSON PLAN

Objectives:

1. To develop an understanding that Jesus was sent to us for a reason.
2. To develop an awareness of the uniqueness of Jesus that even his parents couldn't fully understand.
3. To develop an awareness of Jewish tradition.
4. To show how parents love, worry about and protect their children.
5. To understand that children should love and obey their parents.
6. To follow general and specific directions.
7. To _____.

Theme: We should love and obey God and our parents.

Preparation:

Were you ever lost? How did you feel? As frightened as you were, your parents were probably even more afraid. When a parent finds a lost child, they want to laugh and to cry at the same time because they are so overjoyed. Once Jesus' parents felt like this because of something he did.

Read the story of *Jesus in the Temple.*

Discuss/Ask:

Why did the holy family go to Jerusalem? (Explain customs: i.e., caroling at Christmas, singing "Happy Birthday," going to church.) How do you think Mary and Joseph felt when they realized that Jesus had not returned home with them? What did they do? What would your parents do if you were missing? (Discuss technology and communication differences.)

Mary and Joseph were Jesus' parents on earth. Yet, when they found Jesus in the temple, he said that he had stayed behind to do his father's work. Why do you think this was confusing to Mary and Joseph? How did Jesus show he loved them and his Father in heaven?

Explain:

Jesus returned home with Mary and Joseph. He was a good and loving son, but he was on earth for a very special reason.

Follow Directions for Craft.

JESUS IN THE TEMPLE

FOLD UP

CAREFULLY CUT ARM OF CHAIR

GLUE HERE

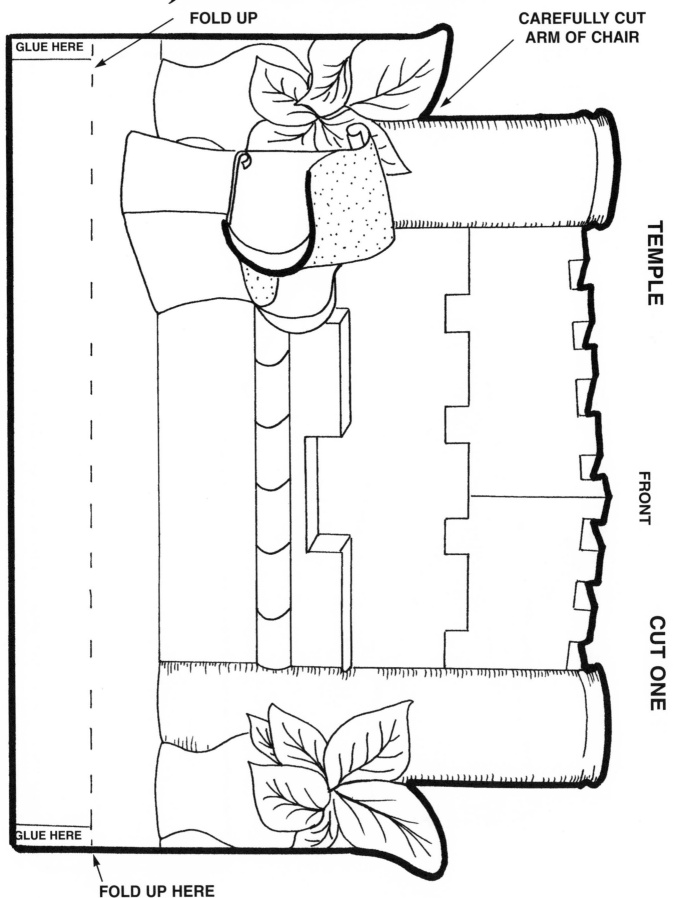

TEMPLE

FRONT

CUT ONE

GLUE HERE

FOLD UP HERE

75

JESUS IN THE TEMPLE

CUT ONE EACH

MARY

GLUE HERE
ATTACH TO TEMPLE FRONT

RIGHT SIDE

ADJUST HERE TO FIT

JESUS IN THE TEMPLE

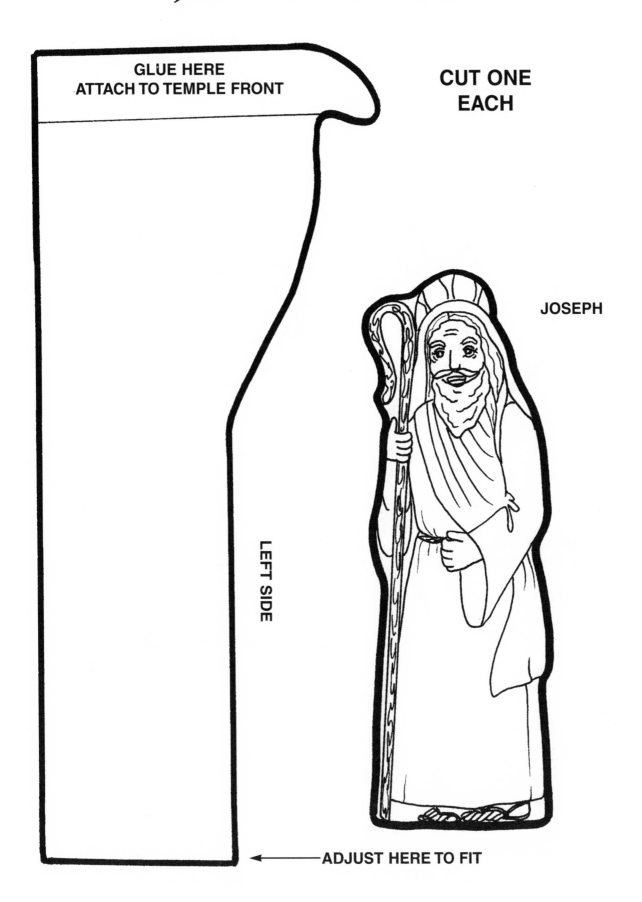

GLUE HERE
ATTACH TO TEMPLE FRONT

CUT ONE
EACH

JOSEPH

LEFT SIDE

← **ADJUST HERE TO FIT**

JESUS IN THE TEMPLE

CUT ONE EACH

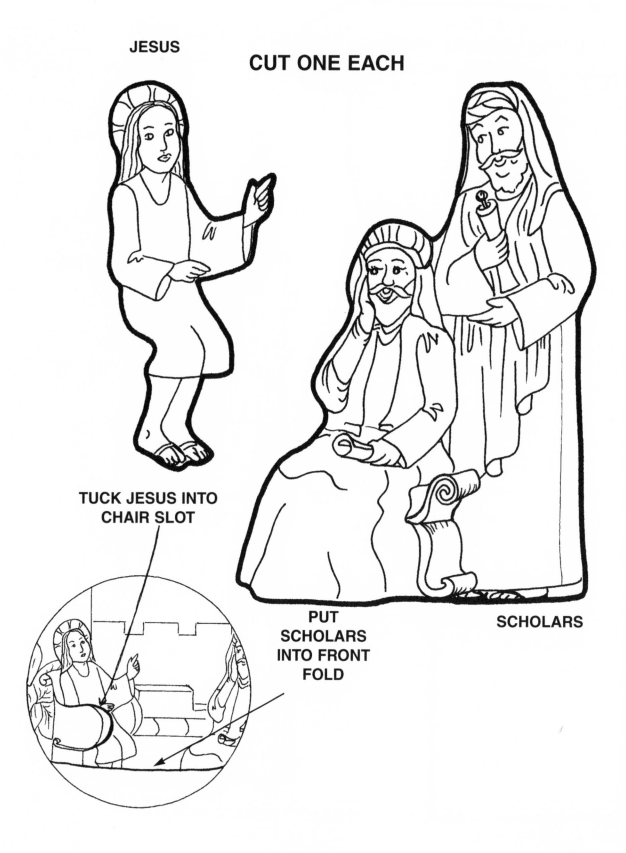

JESUS

TUCK JESUS INTO
CHAIR SLOT

PUT
SCHOLARS
INTO FRONT
FOLD

SCHOLARS

11. THE WEDDING AT CANA

Based on John 2:1-11

Materials

Crayons
Markers or Paints
Scissors
Glue
Tape

Time required: 20–25 minutes

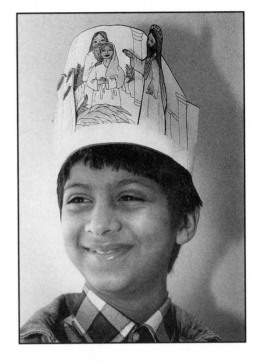

Directions

1. Read story and review lesson.
2. Cut out all pieces on dark lines.
3. Color or paint three wine jugs (one side only). Fold on the line and glue together.
4. Fold up (forward) front of room section to form slot. Glue side edges **only.**
5. Attach sides of headband to the room section. Adjust to fit in back.
6. Slip uncolored jugs into the appropriate slot.
7. Place Jesus in the slot provided, folding arm back.
8. When the arm is folded out (when jugs are blessed) turn the jugs to the colored side.

Suggestions

- Add feathers or tissue paper pieces to the room to give it a festive look.
- Add sequins or glitter to the bride and groom to dress them up.
- Add a piece of yarn to make a belt for Jesus.
- Add scraps of fabric to the clothing.
- Cut out small figures from magazines, or photo of child, to add guests to the wedding.

To Make This Craft Special...

★ Present a clear glass or plastic pitcher of water. Show how clear and sparkling it is. Water is a wonderful gift from God. But, for the special occasion of the wedding at Cana, the people served wine. To make this water change, I have to add something. (Add some red colored, berry-flavored pre-sweetened drink mix.) Jesus was able to change the water by calling on his Father in heaven. **Note:** This can be used as part of the preparation before reading the story.

★ Serve the drink to the children before or while they work on the craft.

★ Play songs with a happy theme.

★ The children may wish to make a small cut-out doll of themselves and friends to add to the sides of the band as if they, too, were wedding guests.

★ If the back of the band is taped closed, it can be opened and the band can be turned inside out for use as a puppet show so that it will appear more like a room.

Send Home

• Send the story *The Wedding at Cana* home with each child so that the sharing and retelling of the story can continue.

• Fold the story and place it in a small box or envelope topped with a bow, as if it were a present for the wedding. Or roll it like a scroll and tie it with a satin ribbon or bow.

THE WEDDING AT CANA

Based on John 2:1–11

There was a wedding at a city called Cana in Galilee. Mary, the mother of Jesus, was one of the guests. Jesus and his disciples (friends) were also invited to the happy event. After a while the wine at the celebration ran out. When Mary saw this, she knew that the people would be embarrassed. She called to Jesus and said, "They have no more wine."

Jesus asked, "What would you have me do?"

Mary knew Jesus could help. She turned to the wedding helpers and said, "Do whatever he tells you."

There were large water jars nearby. Jesus asked the wedding helpers to fill the water jars with fresh water. They did what he said.

Jesus raised his hand over the jars and blessed the water.

Then he told the helpers to take some of the water to the chief waiter and have him taste it. They did what they were told. The waiter in charge tasted the wine and found the wine to be very, very good. He said, "People usually serve the best wine first, then bring out the wine that is not as good later, but this is the best wine. It is wonderful!"

This was Jesus' first miracle.

LESSON PLAN

Objectives:

1. To show the first miracle that Jesus performed and develop an understanding of Jesus beginning his ministry.
2. To show Jesus' obedience to his mother.
3. To show Jesus' love.
4. To understand Jesus' power over nature.
5. To follow general and specific directions.
6. To _____.

Theme: Jesus is a loving, powerful savior.

Preparation:

We don't know much about Jesus when he was growing up. He probably was a lot like the other children growing up in the area. His mother tucked him into bed when he was little and his first bedtime stories were probably the psalms. But, there came a time when Jesus went out into the world and began to fulfill the scriptures. He had to be introduced to the world. Still, he obeyed his mother.

Read *The Wedding at Cana.*

Discuss/Ask:

Have you ever been to a wedding? What do you remember about the wedding? Tell us about the people? A wedding is a happy time; most of the people at the wedding were probably smiling and happy. We want the people getting married to have a very special day. When Jesus and his mother went to the wedding at Cana something happened that could have embarrassed the happy couple. Mary told Jesus of the problem. Jesus showed his love and his obedience. What did he do? Why do you think his mother knew that he would help? Changing the water into wine showed that he had power over nature.

Explain:

Jesus performed his first public miracle that day at Cana by changing water into wine. From that day on people would learn of his love as he traveled the area teaching, preaching and performing other miracles in God's name. Jesus gave the people at the wedding the gift of good wine and he gives us all the gifts of the many parables, stories and lessons of the Bible.

Follow Directions for Craft.

THE WEDDING AT CANA

GLUE

FOLD UP →

GLUE SIDE EDGES ONLY →

GLUE

FRONT

CUT ONE

83

THE WEDDING AT CANA

COLOR "WINE" IN THREE JUGS

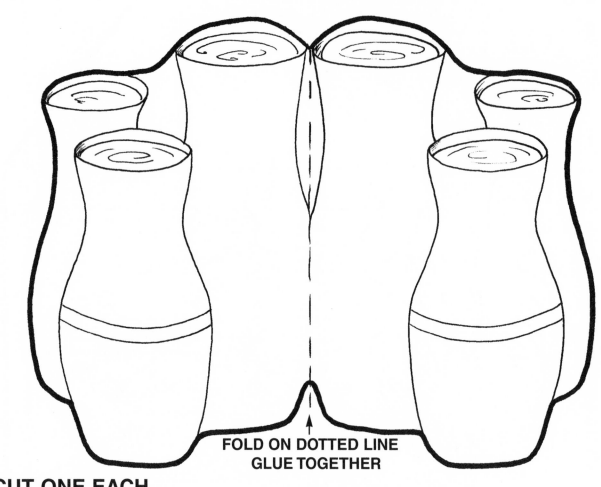

FOLD ON DOTTED LINE
GLUE TOGETHER

CUT ONE EACH

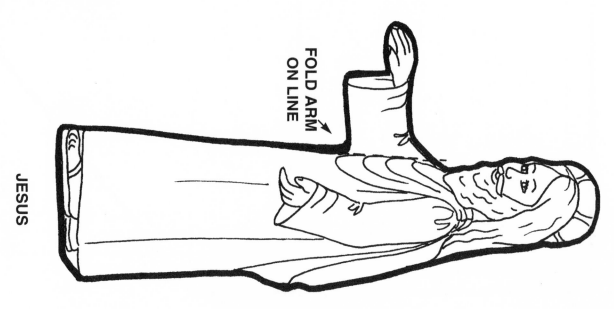

FOLD ARM
ON LINE

JESUS

THE WEDDING AT CANA

GLUE TO FRONT

GLUE TO FRONT

ADJUST AT BACK
GLUE ON PLACE

GLUE TO FRONT PILLARS   **SIDES**   **CUT ONE EACH**

THE WEDDING AT CANA

JUGS WITH WATER

FOLD ARM BACK

JUGS AND JESUS FIT
IN FRONT "TRAY"

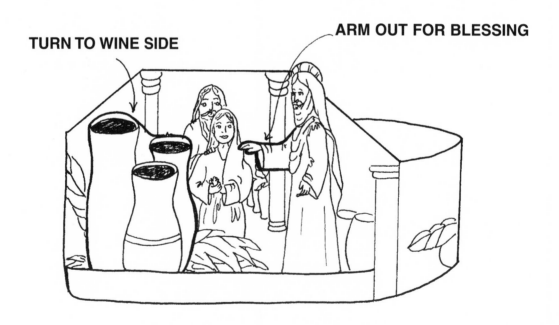

TURN TO WINE SIDE

ARM OUT FOR BLESSING

12. THE MIRACULOUS CATCH

Based on Luke 5:1-11

Materials

Crayons
Markers or Paints
Scissors
2 Brass Fasteners
Hole Punch
Glue or Staples

Time required: 25–30 minutes

Directions

1. Read story and review lesson.
2. Color and decorate all pieces. Cut out.
3. Connect water sections and size to fit. Cut slit in water for boat.
4. Fold net on line and glue together. Use hole punch as indicated.
5. Fold boat on line and insert brass fasteners at sides as shown. (Optional: Glue inside edges *only* of boat before inserting fasteners.)
6. Fold fishermen at line and glue connecting heads only. Arms should be free to fold down over net.
7. When Jesus tells his disciples to lower the net, boat is turned and net is turned. (Note: Design provides for manipulation of pieces that older children would enjoy. For younger children, the net can also be cut on the fold line and one side of net placed on each side of the boat. Then the boat would be turned completely around after the miracle.)

Suggestions

- Glue blue tissue scraps to the water headband.
- Add yarn scraps to beards and hair.
- Glue bits of mesh potato sack to the net.
- Add small fish to the outside of the net as if they are falling out.
- Add glitter to Jesus' halo.

To Make This Craft Special...

★ Turn headband inside out and do the puppet show with the boat inside the circle. Hold the opposite side of the headband and shake slightly. The boat will appear to "bob" up and down in the water.

★ Act out the story using a hammock as a net and stuffed toys as fish. The teacher can use the empty hammock to symbolically wrap around several children to show "catching people."

★ If *The Miraculous Catch* is to be used as a hat only, glue Jesus in the boat on the side with the surprised disciples. Cut the net at fold (as noted in directions). Make one side of the boat for the "empty net" side of the story and one side for the "full net." Glue disciples into the boat. The boat can be taped in place with a rolled piece of tape and turned during the story.

★ Play songs about Jesus' love while the children are working.

Send Home

• Send the story *The Miraculous Catch* home with each child so that the sharing and retelling can continue.

• Roll the story and seal with a fish sticker. Or use a strip from a mesh potato, onion or orange bag (like a net) to tie the scroll. Or fold the story and tuck it into the boat with the disciples.

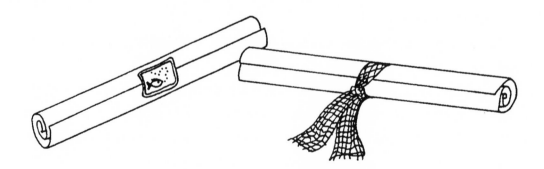

THE MIRACULOUS CATCH

Based on Luke 5:1-11

One morning Jesus was walking along the shore of Lake Gennesaret. A crowd, wanting to hear him speak, pushed close around him. Nearby there were two fishing boats. The men from the boats were washing their nets. Jesus got into one of the boats, the one belonging to Peter. He continued to teach the crowds from the boat.

When Jesus had finished speaking, he said to Peter, "Go out into deep water and let down your nets for a catch."

Peter said, "Master, we have been working all night long and have caught nothing. But since you say so, I will lower the nets."

So they went out into the deep water and lowered the nets. In seconds the nets were filled with fish. The catch was so great that the nets were about to break. Peter called to his friends in the other boat to come and help. That boat too was quickly filled with fish. Soon both boats were so full that they were nearly sinking!

At the sight of this, Peter and the other fisherman were surprised and confused. Peter fell to his knees and begged Jesus to forgive him. He was ashamed that he had doubted Jesus.

Jesus answered him kindly. Jesus told Peter to get up and follow him. "Do not be afraid, " Jesus said. "From now on you will be catching people instead of fish."

When they came to the shore, Peter and the fishermen left their things—their homes, their boats and their nets—and followed Jesus.

This is how Jesus called the first disciples.

Trust in God.

LESSON PLAN

Objectives:

1. To show Jesus' power over the elements.
2. To show that Jesus called common people to be his helpers.
3. To understand why Jesus said that from now on the disciples would be "catching people."
4. To show the loving kindness and understanding of Jesus.
5. To show the trust we should have in Jesus.
6. To follow general and specific directions.
7. To _____.

Theme: Trust in the Lord.

Preparation:

Sometimes we are asked to do something that we think is too hard or not worth trying. At times we want to just give up. Grown-ups can feel that way too. But Jesus is always there for us. He loves us and proves that if we trust in him great things can happen.

Read the story *The Miraculous Catch.*

Discuss/Ask:

When Jesus told his disciples to go back out and drop the nets into the sea, they were doubtful that anything would happen. After all, they had been fishing all night and had caught nothing. Do you think Jesus was testing their trust in him? They hesitated, but did what Jesus said. He performed a miracle. Do you ever hesitate to do what Jesus wants you to do? The fishermen were not rich or famous people; they were people just like all of us. Yet Jesus chose them to spread the word of God. Can we all help to spread the message of God's love?

Why did Jesus tell his friends that from now on they would be "catching people?" (They understood the sea and terms about the sea.) They would be preachers and teachers of his love and not just fishermen anymore.

Explain:

We can all show God's love. We can trust in him and start "catching people" for God. We can be disciples.

Follow Directions for Craft.

THE MIRACULOUS CATCH

**CUT
ONE
EACH**

HOLE PUNCH

GLUE TOGETHER

WHEN DRY, PUNCH HOLES AT ENDS AS SHOWN

HOLE PUNCH

NET

FOLD LINE →

JESUS

OPTIONS: Instead of turning the net around, the net may be cut on the fold line. Place the net without the fish on one side of the boat and the full net on the other side. Turn the boat completely around for the beginning and the end of the story.

THE MIRACULOUS CATCH

CUT ONE

FOLD LINE

GLUE TOGETHER AT HEADS ONLY

INSERT IN BOAT

THE MIRACULOUS CATCH

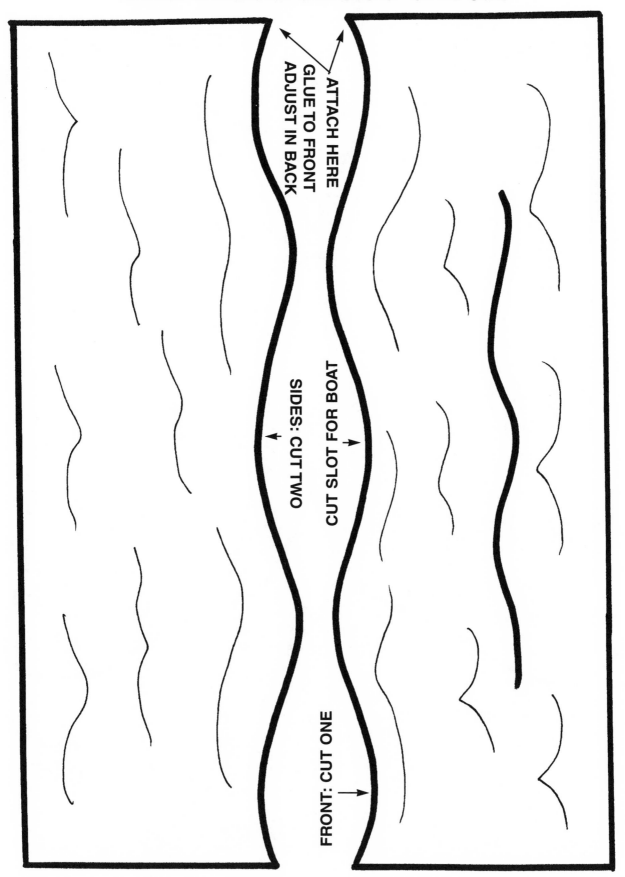

ATTACH HERE
GLUE TO FRONT
ADJUST IN BACK

CUT SLOT FOR BOAT

SIDES: CUT TWO

FRONT: CUT ONE

THE MIRACULOUS CATCH

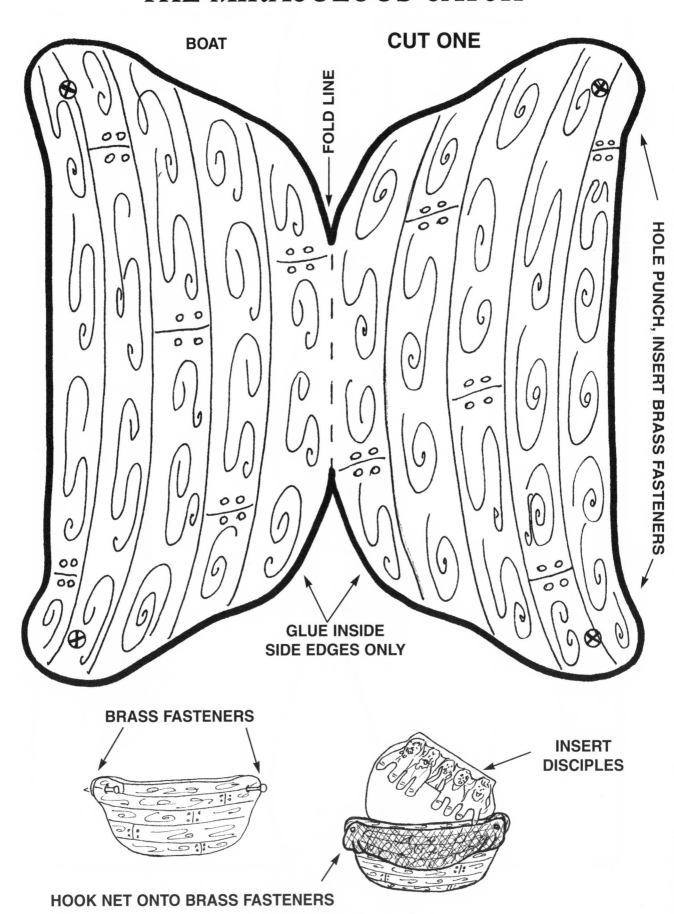

BOAT

CUT ONE

FOLD LINE

HOLE PUNCH, INSERT BRASS FASTENERS

GLUE INSIDE
SIDE EDGES ONLY

BRASS FASTENERS

INSERT
DISCIPLES

HOOK NET ONTO BRASS FASTENERS

94

13. THE LOAVES AND FISHES

Based on Mark 6:30-44

Materials

Crayons
Markers or Paints
Scissors
Glue/Staples

Time required: 20–25 minutes

Directions

1. Read story and review lesson.
2. Color and decorate all pieces. Cut out. (Stand is optional, but useful for puppet show.)
3. Fold up the bottom front piece. Glue at the edges.
4. Attach the sides of hat to front so that the crowds on the side pieces are on *inside.*
5. Place boy with loaves and fishes in the front fold.
6. Jesus' arm can fold up to bless the loaves and fishes.
7. At the end of the story, place basket tab into the slot below the middle apostle's belt to show baskets full of bread collected after the crowd is fed.

Suggestions

- Add bits of cloth to clothing, scraps of yarn for hair.
- Add sand. Thin some white glue and apply it to the foreground with a brush; sprinkle sand on the glue.
- Add glitter to Jesus' halo.
- Add tufts of green tissue for grass.

To Make This Craft Special...

★ After reading the story, share a snack. Use wicker baskets or plates to have the children serve "gummi" fish and crackers. Explain that when we eat our snacks, they will be gone. Imagine what it would be like if, after we served our food, we had lots and lots left over. Compare this to listening to God's word in the readings at church. When we listen and take the readings to our heart, the love expands. We have more than we started with.

★ Play happy songs of hope and joy while the children are working.

★ If *The Loaves and Fishes* is to be used as a hat only, glue the pieces in place, cutting off the stand for the disciples or folding it up out of the way. Glue the disciples to the side of Jesus. Place the basket in front of the disciples. Glue the boy with the loaves and fishes to the front of Jesus off to the side.

Send Home

• Send the story *The Loaves and Fishes* home with each child so that the sharing and retelling of the story can continue.

• Scroll the story and tie a ribbon to close. Put a fish sticker on the end of the ribbon or use a sticker showing happiness in God's word, (i.e., "Joy," "Love," "Thanks Be to God," et cetera)

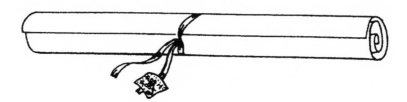

THE LOAVES AND FISHES
Based on Mark 6:30-44

Jesus and the apostles got in a boat to go off to a quiet place.

The people saw Jesus and followed along on the shore, waiting for him to get out of the boat. More and more people gathered.

He saw the large crowd of people and felt sorry for them. They were like little lambs. They needed someone to love them and to lead them. He got out of the boat and began to teach the people. He spoke to the crowd for a long time.

After a while, the apostles came to Jesus with an idea. "There is no food at this place and it is getting late. Why don't you send the people on their way so that they might get something to eat?"

"You feed them," Jesus answered.

The disciples were surprised. They knew it would take a lot of food to feed the people and a lot of money to buy the food. They did not have a lot of money.

"It would take too much to feed all of these people," they said.

"How much food do you have?" Jesus asked.

The disciples went through the crowd looking for food. They found five barley loaves and two fish.

Jesus told the apostles to have the people sit down on the green grass. Taking the food into his hands, Jesus raised his eyes to God and blessed it. He broke the bread. He told his disciples to give it to the people. He divided the fish and gave them to the disciples too. They passed fish out to all the people. Everyone ate until they were full. They couldn't eat any more.

When the people were done eating, the disciples gathered up what was left. There was enough bread to fill twelve baskets and even some fish were left over. Over five thousand were fed that day. It was truly a miracle.

Jesus fed their bodies and their souls.

Jesus, the shepherd, loves us.

LESSON PLAN

Objectives:

1. To show Jesus' love as he calls on God to perform a miracle to feed his people.
2. To understand the importance of trust.
3. To show that Jesus provides for all people.
4. To understand that the body and the soul both hunger.
5. To follow general and specific directions.
6. To _____.

Theme: Trust in God; he will provide.

Preparation:

Jesus went from town to town preaching and teaching. He wanted all people to understand God's love.

Read the story *The Loaves and Fishes.*

Discuss/Ask:

Let's talk about the people who came to listen to Jesus. Why did they come to hear him speak? Why did so many people come? When it got late, why didn't Jesus send all of the people on their way? After Jesus blessed the loaves and fishes, he was able to feed the people and still have so much food left over. How do you think everyone felt after they saw this? Jesus performed a miracle. Why do you think he did this? If Jesus was coming to our town, what would you want to talk to him about? We have questions we would like to ask Jesus because there are many things we don't understand. Even if we can't see God, we can pray and God will always be there for us.

Explain:

Bodies are hungry for food. Souls are hungry for the word of God. When we go to church and listen to the readings, we know that God is talking to us through them. Our hearts are overflowing with his love just like the baskets were overflowing after he fed the people. He wants us to share in his love.

Follow Directions for Craft.

THE LOAVES AND FISHES

ATTACH TO SIDE HERE

GLUE

GLUE AT SIDES ONLY

GLUE

FOLD UP

ATTACH TO SIDE HERE

FRONT

CUT ONE

ARM CAN FOLD UP FOR BLESSING

JESUS

99

THE LOAVES AND FISHES

SIDES

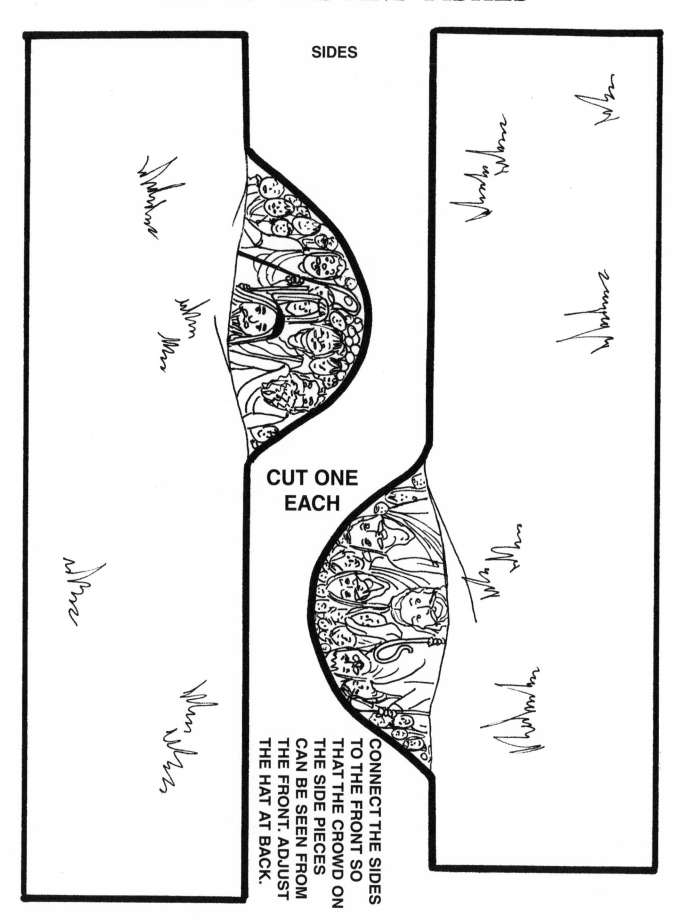

CUT ONE EACH

CONNECT THE SIDES TO THE FRONT SO THAT THE CROWD ON THE SIDE PIECES CAN BE SEEN FROM THE FRONT. ADJUST THE HAT AT BACK.

THE LOAVES AND FISHES

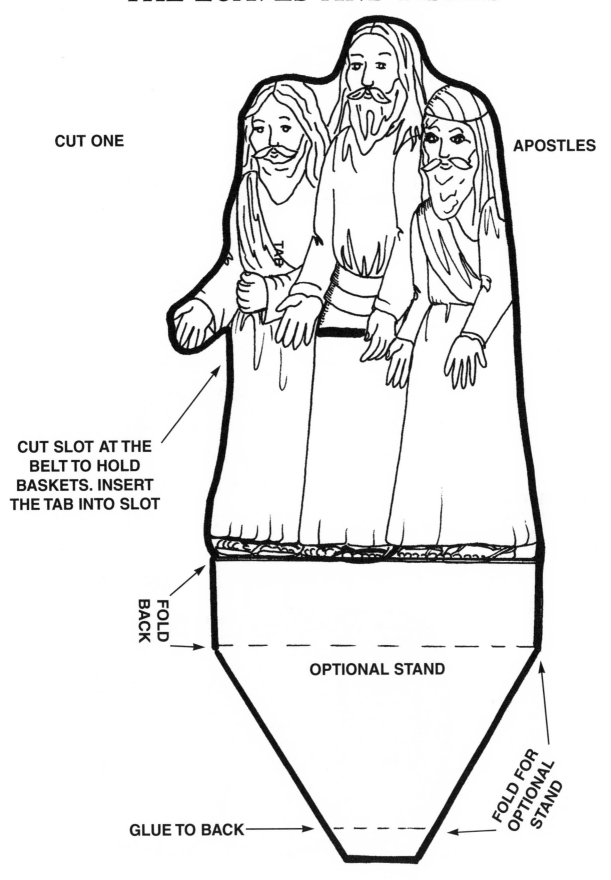

CUT ONE

APOSTLES

CUT SLOT AT THE BELT TO HOLD BASKETS. INSERT THE TAB INTO SLOT

FOLD BACK

OPTIONAL STAND

FOLD FOR OPTIONAL STAND

GLUE TO BACK

THE LOAVES AND FISHES

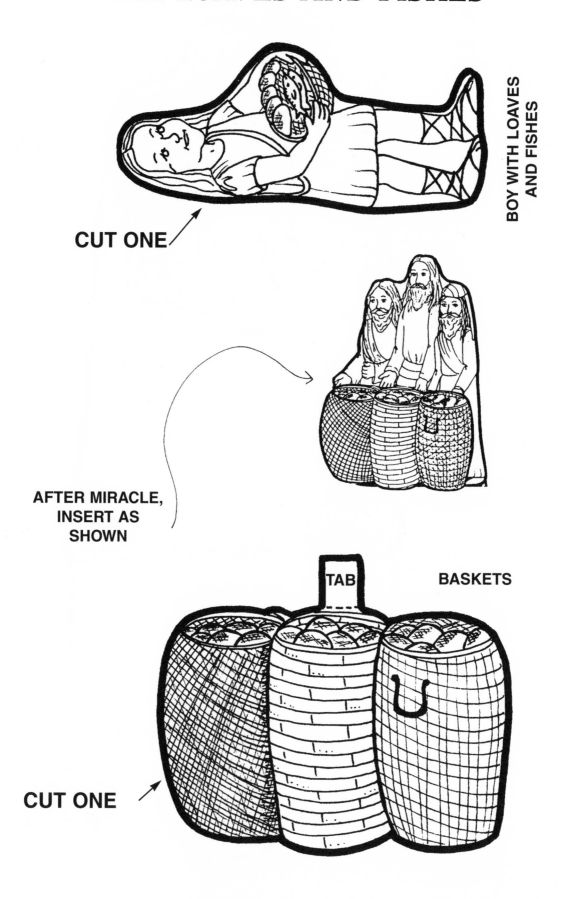

CUT ONE

BOY WITH LOAVES AND FISHES

AFTER MIRACLE, INSERT AS SHOWN

TAB

BASKETS

CUT ONE

14. JESUS WALKS ON THE WATER

Based on Matthew 14:22-33

Materials

Crayons
Markers or Paints
Scissors
Glue/Staples
Tape

Time required: 20–25 minutes

Directions

1. Read story and review lesson.
2. Color pieces. Cut out. Cut slits on water front section to hold the boat and Peter.
3. Glue side waters to front to form band. Adjust at back.
4. Glue sides of boat **only** so that a formed "pocket" results.
5. Glue or tape stands to back of Jesus and Peter.
6. Water peaks are up for storm, down for calm.

Suggestions

- Add pulled cotton balls to the water peaks to make foam.
- Add scraps of cloth to clothing and bits of yarn to hair.
- Add glitter to Jesus' halo.
- Color the boat by laying it open over a textured surface like a brick and running the crayon over it back and forth to create a wooden look.

To Make This Craft Special...

★ Present a pan of water and have the children rest their hands on the surface so that they can see that it could not support their weight. Place a stone on the water and watch as it sinks.

★ Have children act out the story.

★ While the children are working, play songs that show Jesus' love for us all.

★ If *Jesus Walks on the Water* is to be used as a hat only, have the children glue the pieces in place. Jesus should be on the water and reaching for Peter as the disciple is slipping into the water.

Send Home

• Send the story, *Jesus Walks on the Water,* home with each child so that the sharing and retelling can continue.

• Roll the story or fold the story and slip it into the "pocket" of the boat with the disciples.

JESUS WALKS ON THE WATER
Based on Matthew 14:22-33

One day Jesus was talking to a large group of people. When he got done, he sent them on their way. Then he told his disciples to go out in a boat without him. He wanted to be alone for a little while.

Jesus went to the mountains to pray. As evening came, the disciples were still out in the boat—far out on the lake. The wind started blowing hard and the waters began to toss the boat. Even though they were very good fishermen, the winds drove them off their course, making them worried.

As morning came, Jesus saw them tossing about in the boat. They were trying to row against the strong wind. The path to the disciples led right across the water. Jesus began to walk towards them on the water. When the disciples saw him walking on the lake, they yelled, "It is a ghost!" They started to cry out in fear. Jesus tried to calm them.

He called to the disciples, "Take heart; it is I. Do not be afraid."

They knew they were safe when they heard Jesus' voice.

Peter wanted to be near Jesus and called, "Is it really you? Lord, let me come to you."

Jesus told him, "Come; walk to me."

Peter stepped down upon the water and began to walk toward Jesus. Suddenly Peter became frightened to be walking on the water. The winds and waves around him added to his fear. He began to doubt and worry.

Peter cried, "Lord, help me! Save me!"

Jesus reached out his hand to Peter. He said, "Oh, where is your faith? Why do you doubt?"

Jesus held onto Peter and walked with him back to the boat. They got into the boat and the wind stopped.

The people in the boat said, "Truly you are the Son of God."

Trust in the Lord.

LESSON PLAN

Objectives:

1. To show that Jesus had power over nature.
2. To show that a miracle is something we do not fully understand.
3. To understand that we need to have faith in God's love.
4. To show that God always loves us, even when we fail.
5. To follow general and specific directions.
6. To _____.

Theme: Have faith! Trust in God's love.

Preparation:

Jesus loved his disciples, but He knew they were people and would, therefore, make mistakes. He knew that some day he would not be with them. They needed to be teachers of his love and they needed to be strong. They had always been around the sea and understood the sea, so he used the water to teach them.

Read the story *Jesus Walks on the Water.*

Discuss/Ask:

Why do you think Jesus started to walk across the water to the disciples?
Why did Peter want to walk on the water too? Why did Peter start to fall into the water? What did Jesus do to prove his love? What did Jesus do to show that he had power over nature?

Are we sometimes like Peter? We love God, but we start to have worries or question things. God has given us many things to help us. Let's name some things and people that help us get closer to God. (Our parents, teachers, the Bible, stories and parables, et cetera) We can use all of God's gifts to get closer to him.

Explain:

God will always be there for us. We need to have faith in him. He loves us. He knows we all make mistakes, but his love is never ending.

Follow Directions for Craft.

JESUS WALKS ON THE WATER

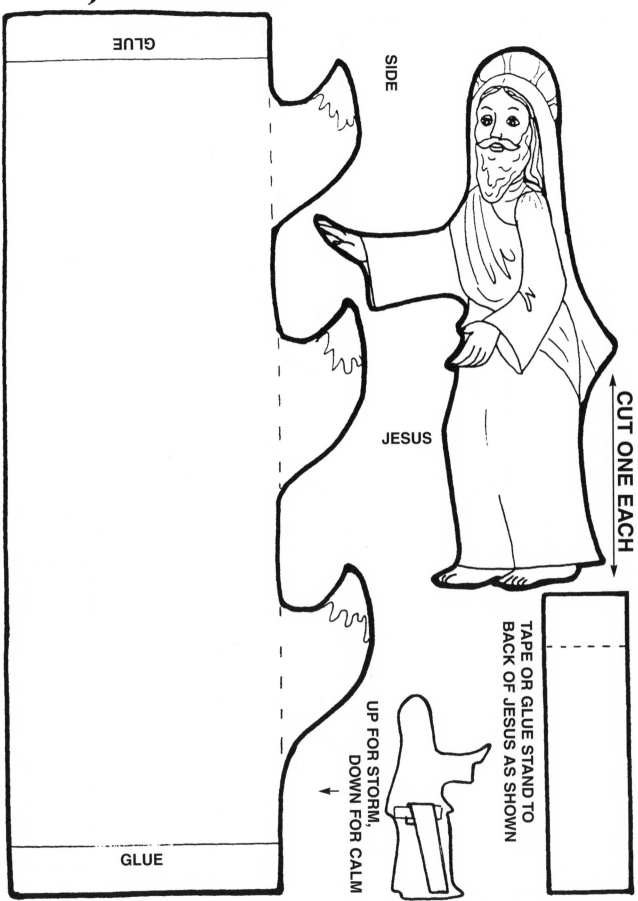

GLUE

SIDE

JESUS

CUT ONE EACH

TAPE OR GLUE STAND TO
BACK OF JESUS AS SHOWN

UP FOR STORM,
DOWN FOR CALM

GLUE

JESUS WALKS ON THE WATER

CUT ONE EACH

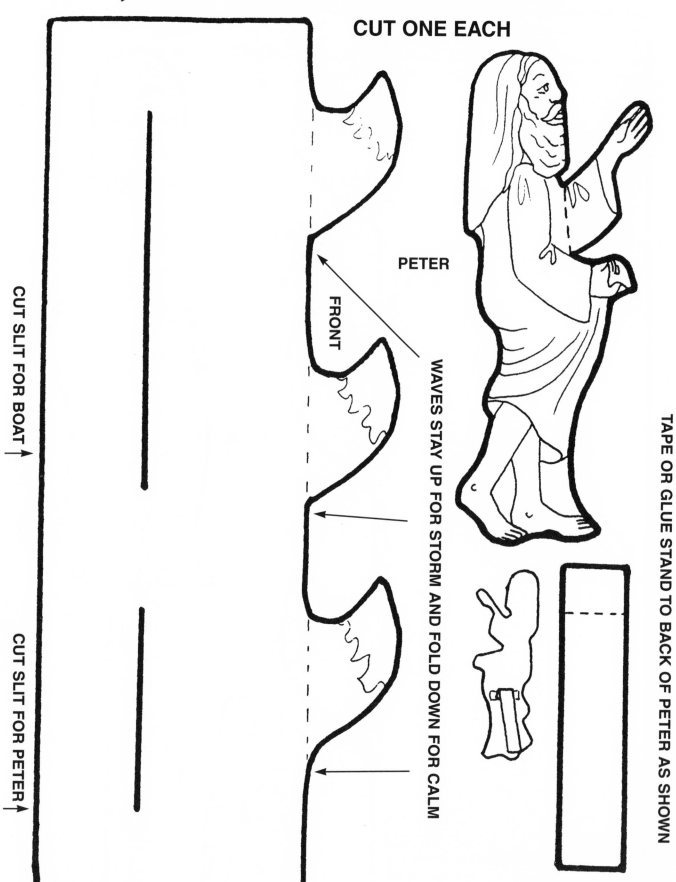

CUT SLIT FOR BOAT →

CUT SLIT FOR PETER →

FRONT

WAVES STAY UP FOR STORM AND FOLD DOWN FOR CALM

PETER

TAPE OR GLUE STAND TO BACK OF PETER AS SHOWN

JESUS WALKS ON THE WATER

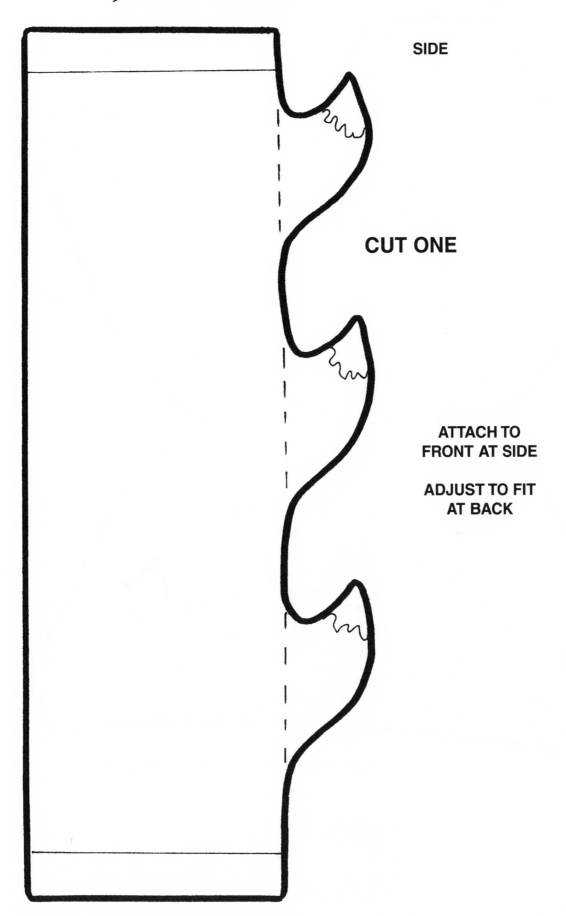

SIDE

CUT ONE

**ATTACH TO
FRONT AT SIDE**

**ADJUST TO FIT
AT BACK**

JESUS WALKS ON THE WATER

CUT ONE

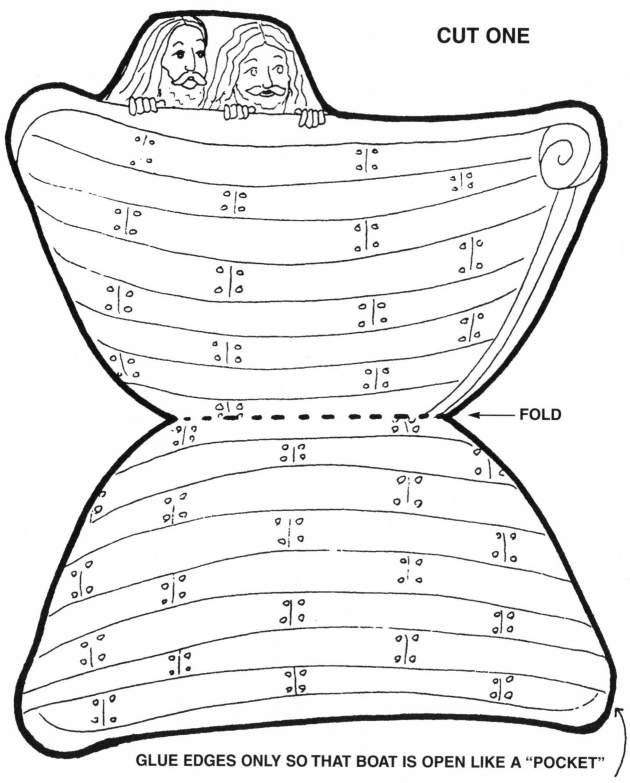

← **FOLD**

GLUE EDGES ONLY SO THAT BOAT IS OPEN LIKE A "POCKET"

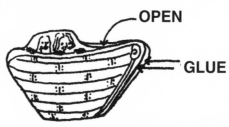

OPEN

GLUE

15. JESUS BLESSES THE LITTLE CHILDREN

Based on Mark 9:33-37, and Luke 18:15-17

Materials

Crayons
Markers
Scissors
Glue/Staples

Time required: 20–25 minutes

Directions

1. Read story and review lesson.
2. Color pieces. Cut out. Carefully cut out the dark lines above rocks.
3. Fold *back* the center bottom piece at fold line.
4. Connect the headband pieces, sizing to fit. Be careful to secure the center bottom piece that is folded up so the slot stays in place (this will hold the disciples when this is used as a puppet show).
5. Fold Jesus' arms so that they can "hug" the child/children.

Suggestions

• Add tiny stones or pebbles to the rocks.
• Add scraps of tissue paper to make grass.
• A tissue scrap or piece of yarn can be added to the clothing to make a sash, robe or belt.
• Use scraps of yarn for hair.
• Add glitter to Jesus' halo.

To Make This Craft Special...

★ A full-body snapshot photo of the child could be incorporated into the story with the paper figures already presented.

★ Songs such as "Jesus Loves the Little Children" can be sung.

★ Act out the story.

★ If *Jesus Blesses the Little Children* is to be used as a hat only, glue the pieces in place. The disciples should be glued to the band off to the side behind Jesus or placed in the slot behind Jesus. Glue the children behind the rock area. Rolled tape can hold the single child with the other children or in Jesus' arms.

Send Home

• Send the story *Jesus Blesses the Little Children* home with each child so that the sharing and retelling can continue.

• Roll the story like a scroll and seal closed with a heart sticker to represent the love of Jesus.

JESUS BLESSES THE LITTLE CHILDREN
Mark 9:33-37

When Jesus spoke to his disciples, He showed the special love he had for little children.

One day the disciples of Jesus were arguing as to who among them was the greatest. Jesus called the apostles to stand near him. He asked them, "What were you arguing about?"

The apostles got very quiet. They were embarrassed since they were talking about their own greatness. Jesus understood. Jesus said to them, "To be first, you must be last. You must be a servant. You must care for others and serve others."

Then, Jesus called to a child that was near and drew the child to himself.

He said, "When you show love for a child like this, you show your love for me. When you show your love for me, you show your love for God in heaven."

*

Luke 18:15-17

Another time, Jesus had been speaking to a large group of people. He spoke to them for a long time and he was tired. When he stopped, the crowd began to move away. Still, some women with babies came to Jesus to have the babies blessed. Soon some little children came running up to Jesus to be blessed also.

The apostles did not want Jesus to be bothered. They wanted him to rest. They tried to get the children to move away. Jesus stopped the apostles and scolded them. He said, "Do not stop the little children. Let them come to me. For the kingdom of heaven is made of children like this. You must love God like a child loves."

Jesus hugged the children to his heart.

Jesus loves the little children.

LESSON PLAN

Objectives:

1. To show the special love Jesus has for children.
2. To understand that Jesus wants all people to follow him as children of God.
3. To understand the importance of faith like that of the women and children in the story.
4. To see Jesus' compassion.
5. To follow general and specific directions.
6. To _____.

Theme: Love God openly and honestly.

Preparation:

Jesus spent a lot of time speaking to people. He told people of God's special love for them. Many times children were in the crowds that came to listen. Jesus did not just talk to the adults; he spoke to the children too. He loved children and was happy to see them.

Read the story *Jesus Blesses the Little Children.*

Discuss/Ask:

Why do you think the apostles tried to have the children leave Jesus' side?
For his part, Jesus was happy to see the children and scolded the apostles. He told them to let the children come. How did Jesus treat the children? How did he show how much he loved them?

Jesus talked about the children and said, "Such is the kingdom of heaven." What do you think he meant? We know God loves us and we can have faith in his love. When we are kind to our parents, brothers, sisters and neighbors, we show his love.

Explain:

We are all God's children and he loves us. We should love God in return and show by our actions that we love him. When we are kind, loving and understanding of others, we show God's love.

Follow Directions for Craft.

JESUS BLESSES THE LITTLE CHILDREN

CUT ONE

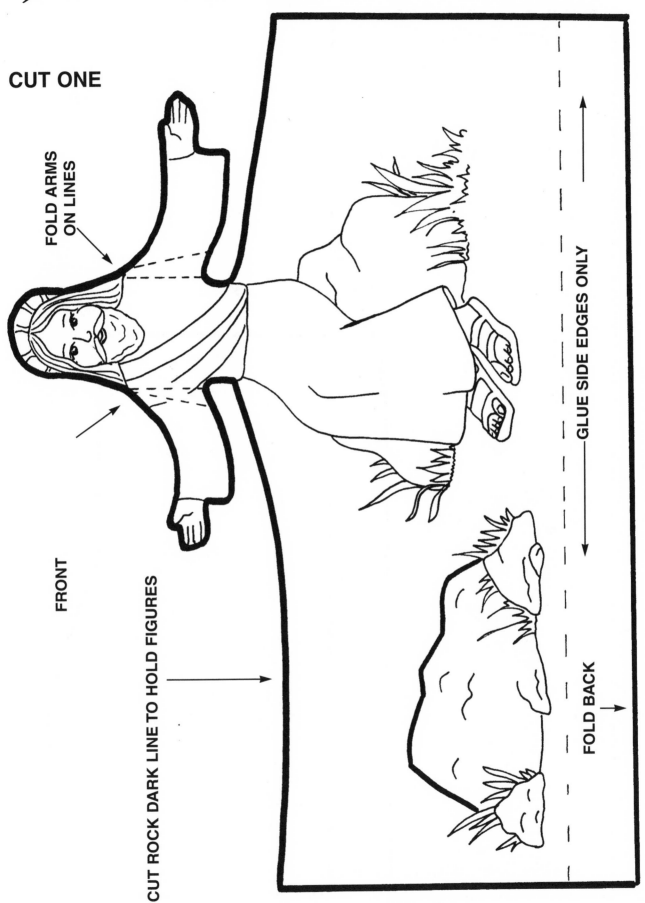

FOLD ARMS ON LINES

FRONT

CUT ROCK DARK LINE TO HOLD FIGURES

GLUE SIDE EDGES ONLY

FOLD BACK

JESUS BLESSES THE LITTLE CHILDREN

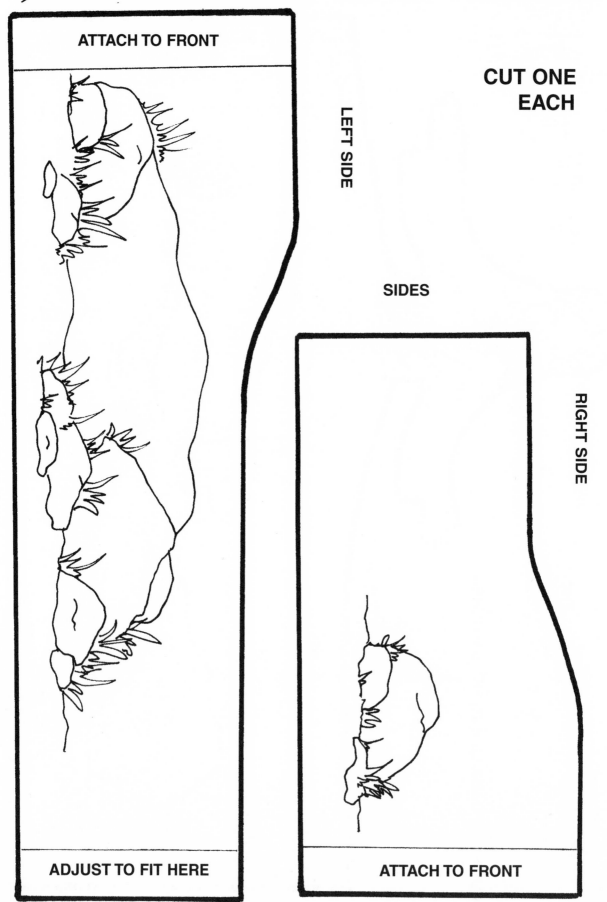

ATTACH TO FRONT

LEFT SIDE

CUT ONE EACH

SIDES

RIGHT SIDE

ADJUST TO FIT HERE

ATTACH TO FRONT

JESUS BLESSES THE LITTLE CHILDREN

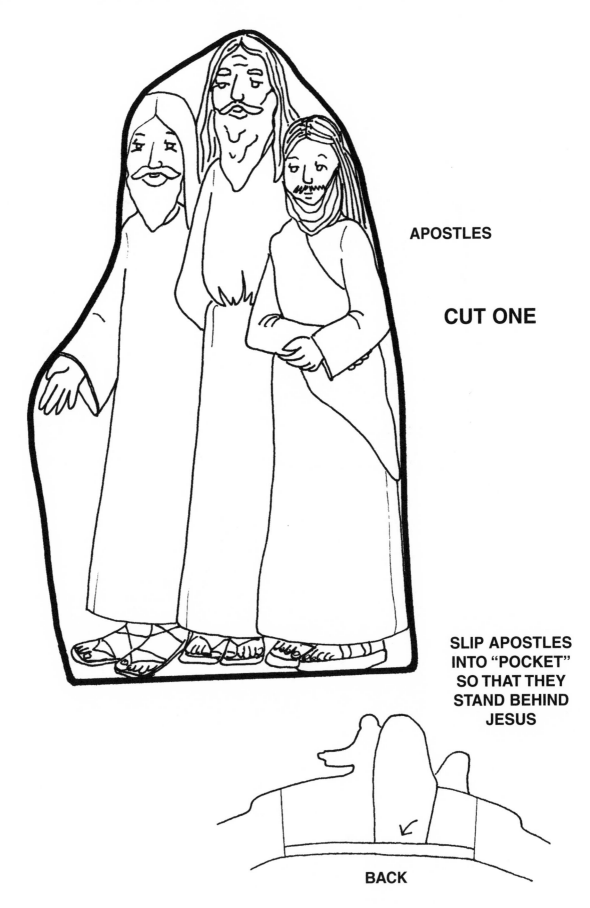

APOSTLES

CUT ONE

**SLIP APOSTLES
INTO "POCKET"
SO THAT THEY
STAND BEHIND
JESUS**

BACK

JESUS BLESSES THE LITTLE CHILDREN

CUT ONE
EACH

CHILDREN

JESUS' ARM
FOLDS TO
EMBRACE
CHILDREN

16. THE GOOD SAMARITAN

Based on Luke 10:29-37

Materials

Crayons
Markers or Paints
Scissors
Glue/Staples
Tape

Time required: 30–35 minutes

Directions

1. Read story and review lesson.
2. Color pieces. Cut out. Cut slot in front. Cut window.
3. Glue sides to front. Adjust at back to fit.
4. Glue the edges of the inn only; place inn on the inside front opposite the road scene so that it is not seen from the front.
5. The robbed man can be put into the slot on the road or onto the donkey's back. He can also be "carried" by the Samaritan and placed in the inn (window).
6. Use stands when pieces are used as a puppet show.

Suggestions

- Add small bits of stone or gravel to road.
- Add scraps of yarn for hair and donkey's tail.
- Add scraps of cloth for clothing.
- Add yarn to make a lead for the donkey.
- Add scraps of green tissue to the trees to make palm leaves.

To Make This Craft Special...

★ Play songs with themes of love while children are completing activity.

★ Have the children help compose a letter that the robbed man might write after he got better, thanking the Samaritan for his kindness. Show how the two might form a friendship and continue to correspond with each other. Stress how they would be a good example to others around them.

★ Act out the story of the Good Samaritan so that the children can see and feel how Jesus was trying to change the old stereotypes with his new gospel of love and neighborliness towards all people.

★ After they have acted it out, have the children "interview" the different players in the story, asking why they acted as they did (i.e., to innkeeper: "What did you think when a Samaritan brought a man who was supposed to be his enemy to your inn for care?")

★ If *The Good Samaritan* is to be used as a hat only, have the children glue the pieces in place. The injured man could be glued on the road as if the Samaritan is just discovering him. The Levite and priest then should be glued to the side band as if walking away. The stands can be cut off the donkey and Samaritan. The donkey can be glued to the side in back.

Send Home

• Send home the story *The Good Samaritan* so that the sharing and retelling can continue. All of the pieces will fit into the inn window for easier transit.

• Fold the story and slip it into the window of the inn or provide an envelope for all pieces and the story. Seal with a heart sticker.

THE GOOD SAMARITAN

Based on Luke 10:29–37

Once a man asked Our Lord, "Who is my neighbor?" Jesus answered by telling this parable (story):

A man was on a road going from Jerusalem to the city of Jericho. Robbers grabbed him, stripped him and beat him. They left him half-dead and bleeding. Soon a priest came down the road. He saw the man but he did not stop. He passed by. Next, a Levite came upon the man. He too saw the man and kept going.

Finally, a Samaritan came by, saw the man and felt sorry for him. He helped the man. He cleaned and dressed his wounds. Next, the Samaritan lifted the man onto his donkey and took him to an inn. The next day, he took money from his own pocket and gave it to the innkeeper.

The Samaritan told the innkeeper, "Take care of him. When I come back, I will repay you if you need more money."

When Jesus was done telling the story, He turned to the man. Jesus asked, "Which of these three do you think was a neighbor to the man who had been hurt?"

The man answered, "The one who was kind to him."

Jesus said, "You should be like the Samaritan. Treat all people with kindness. All people are neighbors to one another."

We are all neighbors in God's wonderful world.

LESSON PLAN

Objectives:

1. To show kindness in action.
2. To develop the concept of "charity."
3. To understand how God wants us to treat one another.
4. To understand that we should love our enemies.
5. To understand the term "neighbor."
6. To follow general and specific directions.
7. To _____.

Theme: Every person is our neighbor.

Preparation:

Jesus often told stories to the people who came to listen to him. He knew that people like stories and remember things told to them in this way. This story is a well-known one.

Read *The Good Samaritan.*

Discuss/Ask:

In this parable story, the man who helped the hurt man proved his kindness, his charity. Charity means love. After Jesus told this story he reminded the listeners that it is important for us all to try to be like the Samaritan. God knows that this is not always easy. Sometimes people hurt us or make us angry. Sometimes we don't like someone just because someone else doesn't like that person.

How does God want us to treat others? Why? It is easy to see that the people who live with us and near us are our neighbors, but God wants us to look on all people as our neighbors.

Explain:

We must take care of each other. We must not let mean-spiritedness hurt others. We should treat our family, friends and even our enemies with kindness. When we treat people with kindness and charity we can see that all people, of all races and ideas, are our neighbors.

Follow Directions for Craft.

THE GOOD SAMARITAN

CUT ONE EACH

FRONT

ROBBED MAN

CUT SLOT IN ROAD

(ROBBED MAN SITS IN SLOT)

THE GOOD SAMARITAN

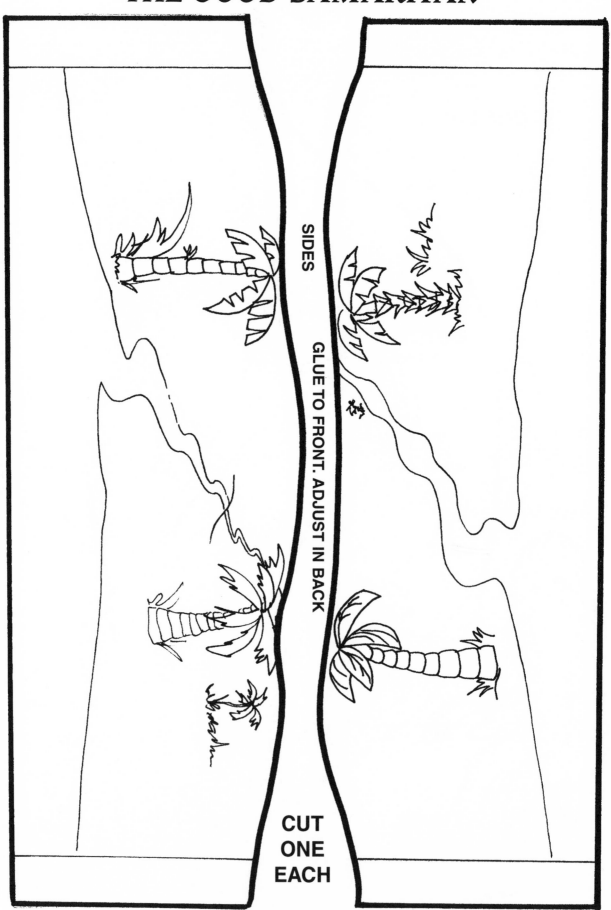

SIDES

GLUE TO FRONT. ADJUST IN BACK

CUT
ONE
EACH

THE GOOD SAMARITAN

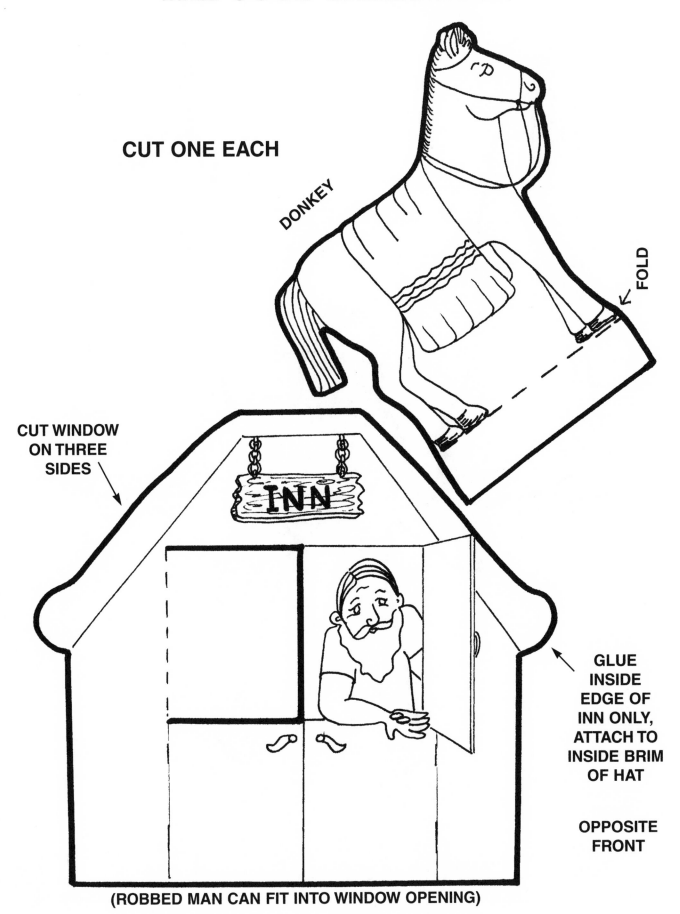

CUT ONE EACH

DONKEY

FOLD

CUT WINDOW
ON THREE
SIDES

INN

GLUE
INSIDE
EDGE OF
INN ONLY,
ATTACH TO
INSIDE BRIM
OF HAT

OPPOSITE
FRONT

(ROBBED MAN CAN FIT INTO WINDOW OPENING)

THE GOOD SAMARITAN

CUT ONE EACH

PRIEST

LEVITE

SAMARITAN

FOLD

OPTIONAL
STAND

126

17. ZACCHAEUS

Based on Luke 19:1-10

Materials

Crayons
Markers or Paints
Scissors
Glue/Staples
Tape

Time required: 20–25 minutes

Directions

1. Read story and review lesson.
2. Color pieces. Cut out. Carefully cut tree to leave a space for Zacchaeus.
3. Fold the front up to form a "tray" for the crowd and Jesus. Glue edges.
4. Attach sides to front.
5. Adjust band to fit at back.
6. A small piece of tape can hold Zacchaeus up in the tree.
7. Roll tape to hold the crowds and Jesus in place.

Suggestions

- Add green tissue paper "puffs" to the tree to resemble leaves. (Pull small squares of tissue over a pencil's eraser end. Put dots of glue on the tree and place the tissue on the glue.)
- Add bits of bark, sticks or tiny stones to the scenery.
- Glitter Jesus' halo.
- Add scraps of cloth to the clothing.
- Add yarn for belts, hair, et cetera.
- Strengthen the band by topping with construction paper.
- Strengthen tree by placing a flat stick or piece of cardboard on the back side of the trunk. Glue or tape in place.

To Make This Craft Special...

★ Have two children hold up a bedsheet, pulling it taut. Have a third child sit on the floor in front of the sheet. Have a fourth child stand behind the sheet and try to guess the expression on the face of the child sitting down. Provide a stool and help the child stand on the stool to look over the sheet in order to see the other child. (You may try the same game, having the sitting child hold an object and the child behind the sheet try to see the object.)

★ If *Zacchaeus* is to be used as a hat only, glue Jesus beneath the tree and use tape to hold Zacchaeus in the tree.

★ Pass out a snack of tiny crackers (like little fish) and big crackers (like graham crackers) and jelly beans, big ones and little ones.

Send Home

• Send the story *Zacchaeus* home with each child so that the sharing and retelling can continue.

• Fold the story very small (4 times). Explain: Here is a little story about a man that wasn't very tall. "When you open up this little page, you will see how a little piece of paper can hold a big story, just like a little person can hold a big idea." Give each child a small, clear bag of tiny jelly beans or a similar very little treat: "Good things come in small packages."

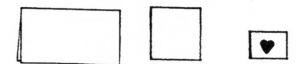

ZACCHAEUS
Based on Luke 19:1-10

Zacchaeus was a tax collector in the city of Jericho. The people did not like tax collectors. They called them sinners.

One day Zacchaeus heard that Jesus was in the town preaching. He thought, "I must see this man Jesus!" But Zacchaeus was a very short man. The crowd was large and the people were so tall that he could not see Jesus. Zacchaeus had an idea. He ran ahead of the crowd and climbed a sycamore tree near the road. Now he could be above the crowd.

When Jesus came under the tree, He looked up and said, "Zacchaeus, come out of that tree. Today I will go home with you and stay in your house."

Zacchaeus was surprised to hear the Lord call him by name. He hurried down out of the tree. He welcomed Jesus to come to his home.

The crowd too was surprised—and a little bit angry! They grumbled and said, "Jesus is going to be the guest of a man who is a sinner."

Jesus paid no attention to the crowd's complaining. He was on earth to save all people.

Zacchaeus stood up as tall as he could. He said, "Lord, I try to be good. The things I have are not just mine. I give half of what I have to help the poor. If I make a mistake or do something wrong to anyone, I repay them four times what I owe them."

This made Jesus happy; he was moved by Zacchaeus. He said, "You and your house are saved. For the Son of Man came to earth to love and save all people."

Jesus loves all people.

LESSON PLAN

Objectives:

1. To have children identify with the concept of "small size in a tall world."
2. To apply a problem-solving technique.
3. To understand the importance of faith in God.
4. To understand the love that Jesus has for us all.
5. To _____.

Theme: Jesus came to save all people.

Preparation:

You are going to hear a story about a man who was not very tall. He was small in size, but his love and faith were great. He had a problem, and he solved it.

Read the story *Zacchaeus*.

Discuss/Ask:

Do you ever feel like you are too small to do something? Do you stand on a stool or step to reach things that are too high on a shelf or in a cupboard? Do you think it was smart of Zacchaeus to climb the tree? Do you think Zacchaeus knew that Jesus was going to stop under the tree? How could you tell? Why was Zacchaeus surprised that Jesus called him? Zacchaeus was a tax collector, and the people called him a sinner. When the people complained that Jesus was going to a sinner's house, how did he answer them? How do we know that Zacchaeus tried to be a good man? How do you think Zacchaeus felt when Jesus decided to come to his house to stay? Do you think Jesus taught the people a lesson about faith and love?

Explain:

Jesus loves all people. He was happy to see that Zacchaeus had faith, even though he had never seen Jesus before. This is the kind of love and faith Jesus wants us to have for him. This is the kind of love Jesus wants us to have when we are dealing with other people. Even though we are small and still growing, our love for Jesus can be great.

Follow Directions for Craft.

ZACCHAEUS

SYCAMORE TREE

FRONT

CUT ONE

ATTACH SIDE HERE

FOLD UP BOTTOM EDGE, GLUE SIDES ONLY

GLUE

ATTACH SIDE HERE

GLUE

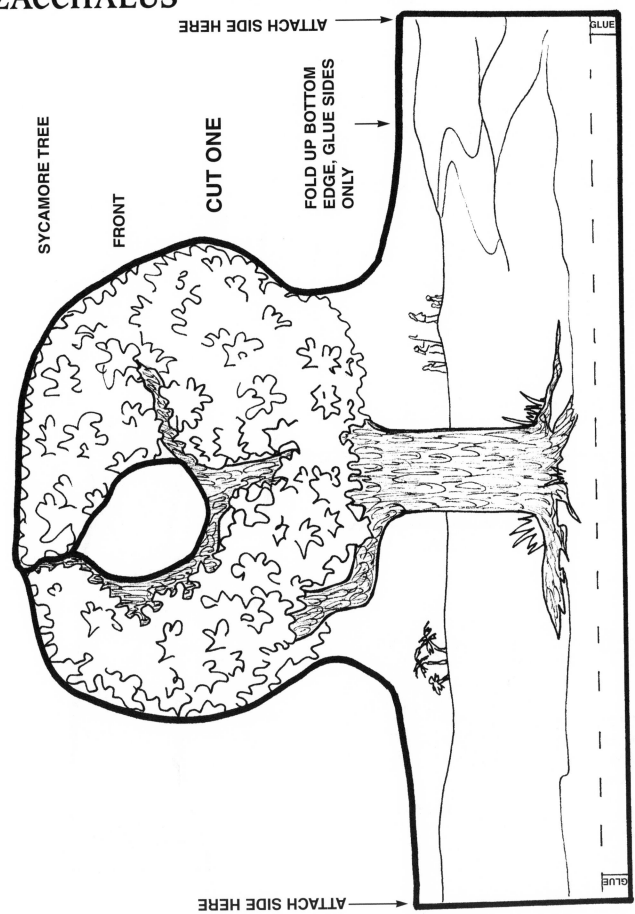

ZACCHAEUS

CUT ONE EACH

CROWD

TUCK JESUS AND CROWD PIECES INTO FRONT "POCKET"

JESUS

132

ZACCHAEUS

CUT ONE EACH

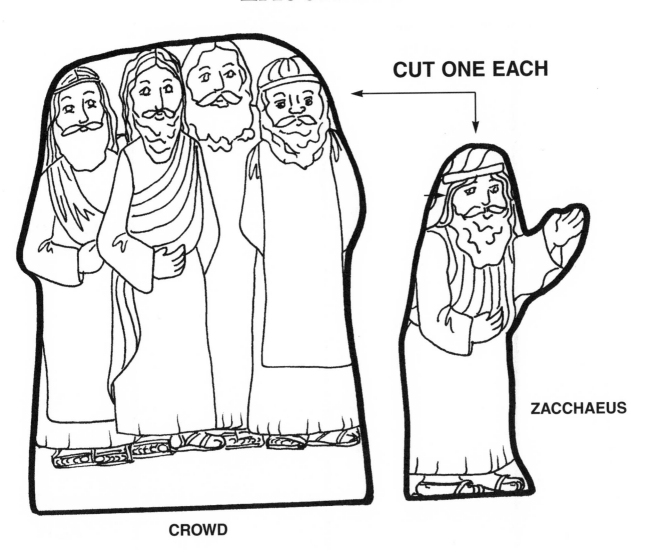

CROWD

ZACCHAEUS

_____

BACK

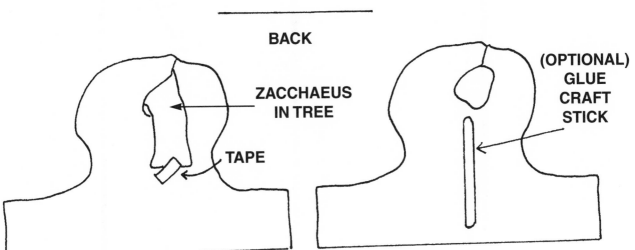

ZACCHAEUS
IN TREE

TAPE

(OPTIONAL)
GLUE
CRAFT
STICK

ZACCHAEUS

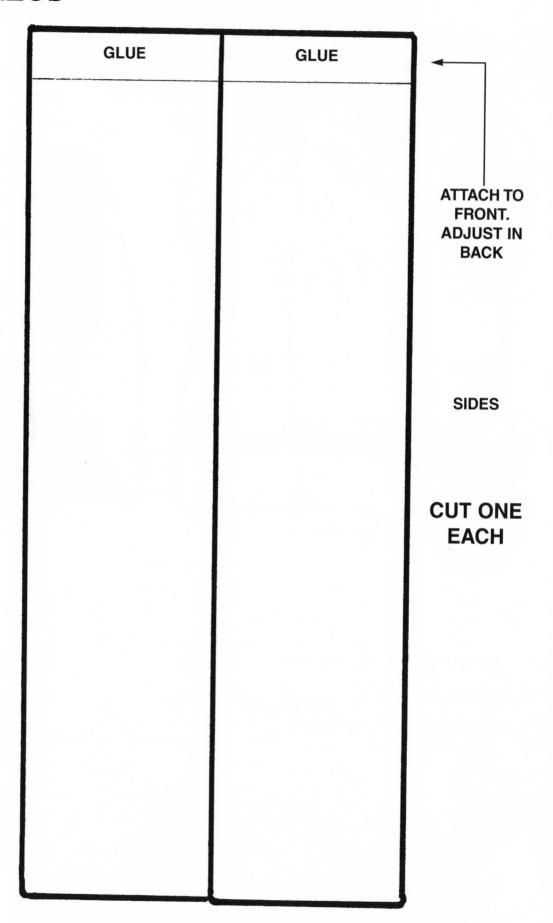

GLUE GLUE

ATTACH TO
FRONT.
ADJUST IN
BACK

SIDES

**CUT ONE
EACH**

134

18. FOUR HELPERS: A PARALYZED MAN CURED

Based on Luke 5:17-26

Materials

Crayons

Markers or Paints

Yarn or String

Scissors

Glue/Staples

Tape

Time required: 30–35 minutes

Direction

1. Read story and review lesson.
2. Color pieces. Cut out.
3. Use a hole punch to make holes on the mat corners and through the helpers' hands. Put yarn through the holes in mat and hands as shown.
4. Glue the front column piece to the front as shown to form a roof opening.
5. Glue or staple the side pieces. Adjust to fit at back.
6. Tuck the paralyzed man into the slits of the mat. Lower the mat through the roof section. Tape helpers temporarily to the roof section for puppet show, permanently for hat.

Suggestions

- Add yarn or hay piece to the mat to give it texture.
- Use yarn, cord or string as rope.
- Add bits of cloth to the clothing.
- Add glitter to Jesus' halo.
- Cover the man on the mat with a tiny piece of sheet material.
- Place a small square of material at Jesus' feet to resemble a rug or flooring.

To Make This Craft Special...

★ Play songs of love and happiness while the children complete the project.

★ Introduce the story with a "trust" game. Put some pillows or stuffed toys on the floor area. Blindfold a child and have him or her maneuver around the objects on the floor as you (slowly and safely) guide them or use verbal signals.

★ If *Four Helpers* is to be used as a hat only, glue the helpers on the roof behind the front scene. Have the mat suspended from the ropes. Roll tape to hold the man on the mat.

Send Home

• Send the story *Four Helpers* home with the child so that the sharing and retelling can continue.

• Place all of the pieces in an envelope for transit home. The opened envelope can be glued to the inside of the hat band.

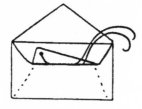
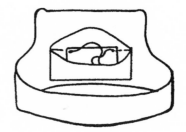

FOUR HELPERS:
A PARALYZED MAN CURED
Based on Luke 5:17-26

One day Jesus was preaching and a large group of people gathered around. They had come from many cities. The crowd grew larger and larger.

After a while, some men came carrying a mat. On the mat lay a paralyzed man. His friends were carrying him so the man could be blessed by Jesus. But the crowd was so large in the building that the men could not get close to Jesus.

Then they had an idea. The men went up on the roof. They removed some of the roof tiles. Next, they carefully lowered the man on the mat down through the hole they had made. The man on the mat came down in front of Jesus. Jesus was moved by their faith. He said, "Friends, your sins are forgiven."

The Pharisees and the teachers were shocked. They wanted to know how Jesus had the power to forgive sin. "This power belongs to God," they said.

Jesus said, "Is it easier to forgive sins or to tell a paralyzed person to walk?" Then, to prove God's power, Jesus turned to the paralyzed man and said, "I say to you, stand up, take up your bed and go home." The man could immediately walk. He went home, and praised God as he went on his way.

All were surprised. They knew that they had seen a miracle.

With Jesus, all things are possible.

LESSON PLAN

Objectives:

1. To show cooperation in action to achieve a goal.
2. To understand the term "trust."
3. To understand the importance of faith.
4. To show the love of God.
5. To show that Jesus heals the body and the soul.
6. To follow general and specific directions.
7. To _____.

Themes: We all need others.
Trust in God, in whom all things are possible.

Preparation:

Have you ever needed the help of a friend? Let's tell about some times that a friend has helped us. Ask the children if they know what it means to be "paralyzed." (Briefly explain.) Let's listen to a story about some people that came to see and hear Jesus. One special person came to see and hear Jesus and was helped by his friends and blessed by Jesus in two special ways.

Read the story *Four Helpers.*

Discuss/Ask:

The friends in the story helped their friend. How do you know from the story that the man on the mat trusted his friends? Why did so many people come to see Jesus? Why did the paralyzed man want to come to see Jesus? The paralyzed man also trusted Jesus. Jesus loved the man and cured him in two ways. How did he help the man? (He cured the man's paralysis and forgave him his sins.) Talk about the crowd's reaction and Jesus' response.

Explain:

The man that came to Jesus could not walk, so he wanted Jesus' help, but he also needed Jesus' love to cure him of his sins. The man trusted his friends and trusted in the Lord. In the same manner, we should be good friends to others, trusting in them and helping them to trust us; but our greatest trust should be in the Lord.

Follow Directions for Craft.

FOUR HELPERS: A PARALYZED MAN CURED

CUT ONE EACH

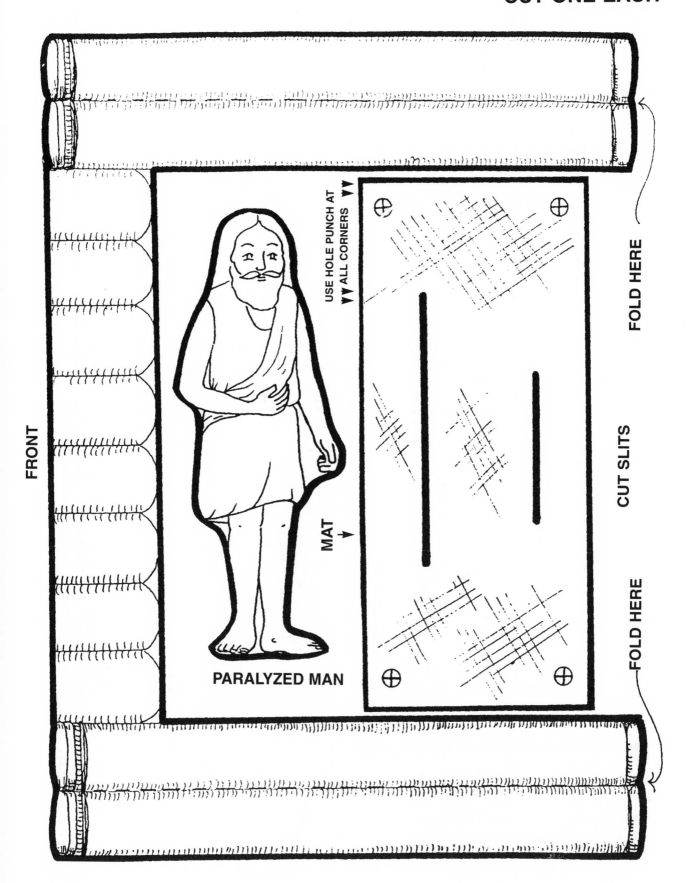

FRONT

FOLD HERE

USE HOLE PUNCH AT
ALL CORNERS

CUT SLITS

FOLD HERE

MAT →

PARALYZED MAN

FOUR HELPERS: A PARALYZED MAN CURED

CUT ONE

GLUE

GLUE SIDE TO FRONT HERE

FRONT II

GLUE

GLUE SIDE TO FRONT HERE

GLUE SIDE
PILLARS TO
FRONT II SO THAT
TOP AWNING
FORMS AN OPEN
ROOF

FOUR HELPERS: A PARALYZED MAN CURED

HELPERS

CUT ONE EACH

USE HOLE PUNCH AT HANDS
LACE YARN THROUGH HOLES

INSERT YARN AS SHOWN

FOUR HELPERS: A PARALYZED MAN CURED

CUT ONE EACH

SIDES

GLUE TO FRONT AT SIDES. ADJUST IN BACK.

ATTACH TO FRONT

ATTACH TO FRONT

19. THE RESURRECTION

Based on Luke 24:1-11

Materials

Crayons
Markers or Paints
Scissors
Glue/Staples
Tape

Time required: 20–25 minutes

Directions

1. Read story and review lesson.
2. Color pieces. Cut out. Fold pieces as marked.
3. Glue the rock section on the sides so that the rock will open like a door.
4. Glue the sides to the front rock section. Adjust hat to fit at back.
5. Roll tape and attach the two angels to the sides of rock section.
6. Fold Jesus in glory and slip into the bottom pocket area of the rock section.
7. "Roll back" the rock, unfold Jesus in glory. He is risen!

Suggestions

- Add glitter to the halo and radiance around the risen Jesus.
- Add glitter to the halos on the angels and Mary.
- Add small feathers to the angel's wings.
- Add small stones or pebbles to the front rock section.
- Add greenery like tissue paper or construction paper strips to the top of tree section.
- Decorate the side strips with tiny stones or greenery pieces to look like plants.

To Make This Craft Special...

★ Bring in, or have the children bring in, symbols of Easter. Stress that symbols such as the lily have a religious significance, unlike symbols such as the Easter bunny and candy, developed later to commercialize the season.

★ Have the children act out the parts of the women at the tomb and the angels, and show how the disciples might have acted after the woman came and told them that Jesus had risen.

★ Play religious Easter songs while the children are completing the project.

★ If *The Resurrection* is to be used as a hat only, glue the pieces in place with Jesus rising and the women to the back, coming towards the tomb. Glue the angels to either side of the entrance.

Send Home

• Send the story *The Resurrection* home with each child so that the sharing and retelling can continue.

• An envelope glued to the inside front of the band behind the tomb can be used to hold the pieces and the folded story.

• Or scroll the story page and hold closed with an Easter sticker or several strands of Easter grass. Or if artificial white baby lilies are available, add these to the tie, explaining that the lily is a sign of Easter joy.

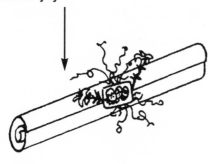 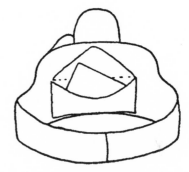

THE RESURRECTION
Based on Luke 24:1-11

Early in the morning on the first day of the week, some women came to Jesus' tomb. As was the custom, they brought spices with them to use on Jesus' body. When they got to the tomb, they saw that it was open. The big stone, which had been like a door to the cave, had been rolled back. They entered the cave. How surprised they were that they could not find Jesus' body there! They were worried and confused. Suddenly they saw two men in shining clothes beside them. The women were afraid and fell to their knees.

The men (who were really angels) said, "Why do you look for Jesus here? He is the living Lord. As you can see, he is not here. He has risen from the dead. You should remember, when Jesus was here he told you all the things that would happen. He said he would be handed over to people who would crucify him on the cross, but in three days he would rise up again. He has done all of this for you."

When the angels talked to them, they remembered that Jesus had told them all of these things before he had died on the cross. Now Jesus had come back to them. He had kept his promise.

He is Risen!

LESSON PLAN

Objectives:

1. To begin to explore the concept of the resurrection.
2. To see God's great love in action and to understand that this love is for all of his people.
3. To see a promise fulfilled.
4. To show that even the people who were close to Jesus didn't understand when he had told them that he would rise again in three days.
5. To follow general and specific directions.
6. To _____.

Theme: God keeps his promise; God is love.

Preparation:

Many people loved Jesus. When he died on the cross they were sad. But then he kept his promise.

Read the story *The Resurrection.*

Discuss/Ask:

Easter reminds us of many things. Let's list some of the things. As much as we like some of the Easter symbols, none of them have any real meaning without the true reason for the season. The only true meaning of Easter is the resurrection. Jesus, and his great love fulfilled, is the reason we celebrate. All of the other symbols were added later. The happy springtime season is Jesus' promise to us. The resurrection is proof of God's great love for us. *Reread the story.*

How do you think the women felt when they went to the tomb and it was empty?

What did the angel tell them? Imagine yourself as one of his disciples back then. What do you think you would feel? Say? Do?

Explain:

Jesus showed his love for us by dying on the cross. God sent his only Son to earth to be born, to live, to die and to rise again to show his love. We should show our love for God every day by living good lives, by praying, loving and sharing.

Follow Directions for Craft.

THE RESURRECTION

CUT ONE

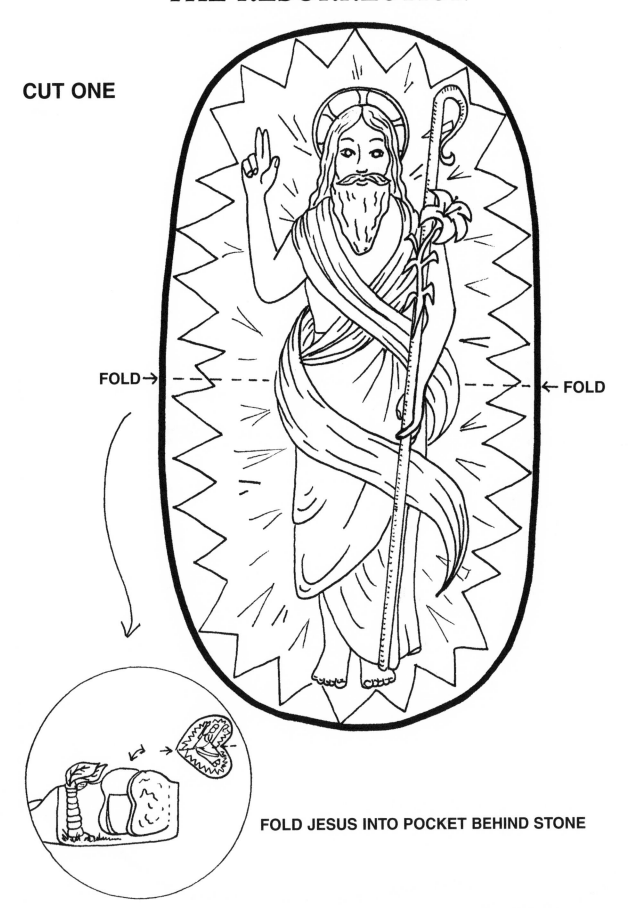

FOLD→ ←FOLD

FOLD JESUS INTO POCKET BEHIND STONE

THE RESURRECTION

FOLD

GLUE AT SIDES ONLY. ALLOW STONE TO OPEN

FRONT

CUT ONE

THE RESURRECTION

ADJUST TO FIT→

SIDE →

CUT ONE EACH

ANGELS

GLUE TO FRONT HERE

THE RESURRECTION

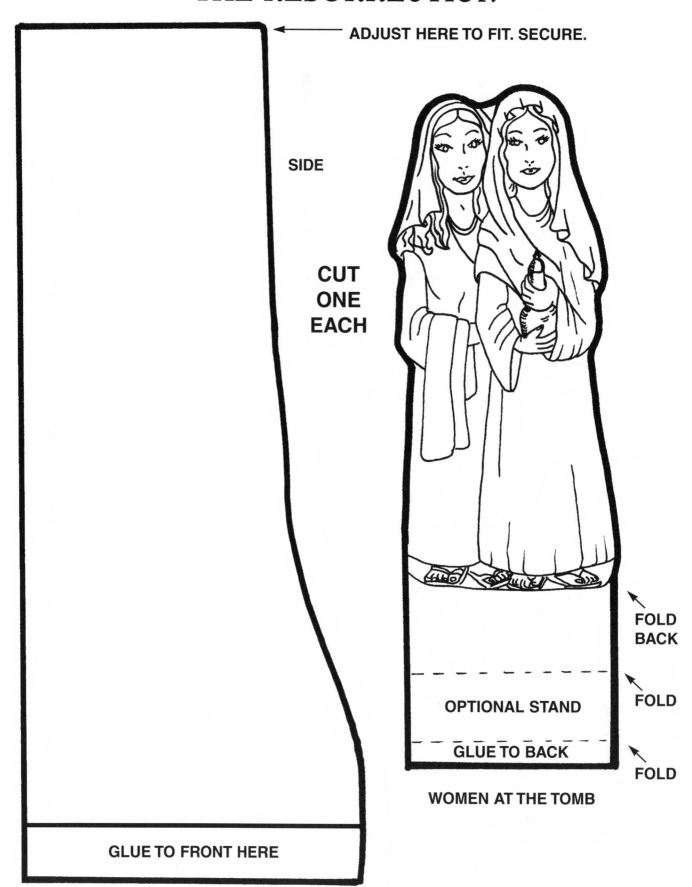

ADJUST HERE TO FIT. SECURE.

SIDE

CUT
ONE
EACH

FOLD
BACK

FOLD

OPTIONAL STAND

GLUE TO BACK

FOLD

WOMEN AT THE TOMB

GLUE TO FRONT HERE